FROM ZERO TO HERO IN DROPSHIPPING WITH SHOPIFY: EVERYTHING YOU NEED TO KNOW TO SUCCEED

Sébastien JULLIARD-BESSON – Digital Workout 2023

Translate from the original work in French « De Zéro à Héros du Dropshipping avec Shopify : Tout ce que vous devez savoir pour réussir »

PREFACE

In a world where digitization has transformed our way of life, work, and business, online commerce has become an unstoppable force. At the heart of this revolution is dropshipping, an online selling method that has allowed thousands of entrepreneurs to start their own businesses with minimal investment. It is in this context that I am delighted to present to you this training, titled 'From Zero to Hero in Dropshipping with Shopify in 2024.'

My name is Sébastien JULLIARD-BESSON, and I am an e-commerce expert with over 15 years of experience in the field. As a Web Project Manager, I have had the opportunity to work on a multitude of online commerce projects and have gained in-depth knowledge of the challenges and opportunities in this ever-evolving sector. It is this expertise that I wanted to share with you through this training.

This training is designed as a comprehensive guide to help you navigate the world of dropshipping with Shopify. It is divided into 21 chapters, each focusing on a different aspect of the process. You will start with an introduction to dropshipping before delving into the details of creating and managing a Shopify store.

You will learn how to choose a niche for your store, find reliable dropshipping suppliers, and efficiently add products to your store. You will also discover how to configure payment and shipping settings, choose and customize a theme for your store, and optimize your store for SEO.

However, creating a successful online store is not just about the technical aspects. That's why this training also covers topics such as marketing, customer service, and performance analysis. You will learn how to create an effective marketing strategy, use email marketing and social media to attract and retain customers, and provide excellent customer service. You will also learn how to handle returns, refunds, and customer reviews, as well as how to use remarketing to increase sales.

Ultimately, this training aims to provide you with a comprehensive understanding of dropshipping with Shopify and equip you with the tools and knowledge you need to succeed. Whether you are a complete beginner or have some experience in online commerce, I am confident that you will find valuable information and practical advice in this training.

Wishing you enriching reading and a successful dropshipping journey,

Sébastien JULLIARD-BESSON

CHAPTER 1: INTRODUCTION TO DROPSHIPPING

1. What is Dropshipping?
2. Why is Dropshipping Popular?
3. How to Start a Dropshipping Business?
4. The Benefits of Dropshipping
5. Challenges of Dropshipping
6. Conclusion

CHAPTER 2: UNDERSTANDING SHOPIFY

1. What is Shopify?
2. How Does Shopify Work?
3. The Advantages of Shopify
4. How to Get Started with Shopify for Dropshipping
5. Shopify and Dropshipping

CHAPTER 3: HOW TO CREATE A SHOPIFY STORE

1. Step 1: Sign up for Shopify
2. Step 2: Setting up Your Store
3. Step 3: Adding Products
4. Step 4: Setting up Payment and Shipping Settings
5. Step 5: Choosing and Customizing a Theme for Your Store
6. Step 6: Optimizing Your Store for SEO
7. Step 7: Setting Up Google Analytics and Facebook Pixel
8. Step 8: Launching Your Shopify Store
9. Conclusion: Successful Launch of Your Shopify Store

CHAPTER 4: CHOOSING A NICHE FOR YOUR SHOPIFY STORE

1. Understanding What a Niche Is
2. Why Choosing a Niche Is Important for Your Shopify Store
3. How to Identify a Profitable Niche
4. Factors to Consider When Choosing a Niche
5. Tools to Help You Find a Niche
6. How to Validate Your Niche Idea
7. Conclusion

CHAPTER 5: HOW TO FIND DROPSHIPPING SUPPLIERS

1. Understanding the Role of Suppliers in Dropshipping

2. Different Platforms for Finding Suppliers
3. How to Contact Suppliers
4. How to Negotiate with Suppliers
5. Common Mistakes to Avoid When Selecting Suppliers
6. Additional Tips for Finding Dropshipping Suppliers
7. Conclusion

CHAPTER 6: HOW TO ADD PRODUCTS TO YOUR SHOPIFY STORE

1. Adding Products via Shopify
2. Adding Products via the Shopify Mobile App
3. Bulk Product Addition
4. Managing Digital Products
5. Using the Shopify API
6. Adding Products via Dedicated Dropshipping Platform Plugins
7. Conclusion

CHAPTER 7: HOW TO SET UP PAYMENT AND SHIPPING SETTINGS ON SHOPIFY

1. Setting Up Payment Settings on Shopify
2. Setting Up Shipping Settings on Shopify

CHAPTER 8: HOW TO CHOOSE AND CUSTOMIZE A THEME FOR YOUR SHOPIFY STORE

1. Why Theme Selection is Crucial for Your Shopify Store
2. How to Choose the Right Theme for Your Shopify Store
3. How to Customize Your Shopify Theme
4. Best Practices for Theme Customization
5. Conclusion

CHAPTER 9: HOW TO OPTIMIZE YOUR SHOPIFY STORE FOR SEO

1. Introduction to SEO Optimization for Shopify
2. The Importance of SEO for Your Shopify Store
3. How to Add Keywords for SEO on Shopify
4. Site Optimization for SEO
5. SEO Checklist for Shopify Online Stores
6. Conclusion

CHAPTER 10: HOW TO SET UP GOOGLE ANALYTICS AND META PIXEL FOR YOUR SHOPIFY STORE

1. Google Analytics Setup
2. Meta Pixel Setup
3. Conclusion

CHAPTER 11: HOW TO CREATE A MARKETING STRATEGY FOR YOUR SHOPIFY STORE

1. Step 1: Situation Analysis
2. Step 2: Define Your Target Audience
3. Step 3: Establish Your Marketing Goals
4. Step 4: Choose Your Marketing Channels
5. Step 5: Impact Analysis
6. Step 6: Review and Adjustment

CHAPTER 12: HOW TO USE EMAIL MARKETING AND SOCIAL MEDIA MARKETING FOR YOUR SHOPIFY STORE

1. Email Marketing for Your Shopify Store
2. Social Media Marketing for Your Shopify Store
3. Conclusion

CHAPTER 13: HOW TO USE INFLUENCER MARKETING AND PAID ADVERTISING FOR YOUR SHOPIFY STORE

1. Section 1: Influencer Marketing
2. Section 2: Paid Advertising
3. Conclusion

CHAPTER 14: PROVIDING EXCELLENT CUSTOMER SERVICE IN YOUR SHOPIFY STORE

1. Understanding Customer Expectations
2. Setting Up Effective Communication Channels
3. Responding to Customer Requests and Complaints
4. Handling Returns and Refunds
5. Personalizing the Customer Experience
6. Building Customer Loyalty
7. Measuring Customer Satisfaction
8. Success Stories of Shopify Stores with Excellent Customer Service
9. Conclusion

CHAPTER 15: HOW TO MANAGE RETURNS, REFUNDS, AND

CUSTOMER REVIEWS IN YOUR SHOPIFY STORE

1. Returns and Refund Management
2. Customer Review Management
3. Conclusion

CHAPTER 16: HOW TO INCREASE THE AVERAGE ORDER VALUE AND CONVERSION RATE IN YOUR SHOPIFY STORE

1. Increasing Average Order Value
2. Increasing the Conversion Rate
3. Conclusion

CHAPTER 17: HOW TO USE REMARKETING TO INCREASE SALES IN YOUR SHOPIFY STORE

1. What Is Remarketing?
2. Why Is Remarketing Important for Your Shopify Store?
3. How to Implement a Remarketing Strategy for Your Shopify Store?
4. How to Optimize Your Remarketing Strategy?
5. Conclusion

CHAPTER 18: ANALYZING AND OPTIMIZING YOUR SHOPIFY STORE'S PERFORMANCE

1. Introduction to Performance Analysis and Optimization
2. Collecting Data for Your Shopify Store
3. Traffic and Visitor Behavior Analysis
4. Product Performance Evaluation
5. User Experience Optimization
6. Marketing Performance Analysis
7. Using Data for Strategic Decision-Making
8. Conclusion

CHAPTER 19: MANAGING GROWTH AND CHALLENGES IN RUNNING A SHOPIFY STORE

1. Inventory and Supplier Management
2. Maintaining High-Quality Customer Service
3. Managing Returns and Refunds
4. Conversion Optimization and Increasing Average Order Value
5. Performance Analysis and Optimization

6. International Growth Management
7. Conclusion

CHAPTER 20: HOW TO STAY UPDATED WITH DROPSHIPPING TRENDS

1. Understanding the Importance of Trends
2. Monitoring Market Trends
3. Analyzing Dropshipping Trends
4. Adapting Your Strategy to Trends
5. Examples of Dropshipping Trends
6. Conclusion

CHAPTER 21: CONCLUSION; HOW TO SUCCEED WITH A DROPSHIPPING SHOPIFY STORE

1. Success Stories
2. Key Elements to Master for Success
3. Common FAQs
4. Additional Resources
5. Conclusion

GLOSSARY

CHAPTER 1: INTRODUCTION TO DROPSHIPPING

1. What is Dropshipping?

Dropshipping is an e-commerce business model that has revolutionized the way products are sold and distributed. In the traditional e-commerce model, a retailer must purchase stocks, store them in a warehouse, and then ship them to customers when they place an order. This requires a significant initial investment in inventory and storage space, as well as ongoing inventory and shipping management.

However, with dropshipping, the retailer doesn't need to manage inventory or shipping. Instead, they partner with a dropshipper - a wholesaler who stocks their own products. When a customer places an order, the retailer forwards the order details to the dropshipper, who then ships the product directly to the customer. The retailer never has to handle the product themselves.

This means that the startup cost for a dropshipping business is much lower than that of a traditional e-commerce business. Additionally, since the retailer doesn't have to manage inventory or shipping, they can focus on other aspects of the business, such as marketing and customer service.

Traditional E-commerce Model:

• The retailer purchases products from the wholesaler.

CHAPTER 1: INTRODUCTION TO DROPSHIPPING 11

• Products are stored in a warehouse managed by the retailer.

• When a customer places an order, the retailer ships the products from the warehouse directly to the customer.

Dropshipping Model:

• The retailer partners with a dropshipper (who is also a wholesaler).

• When a customer places an order with the retailer, the order details are forwarded to the dropshipper.

• The dropshipper then ships the products directly to the customer.

2. Why is Dropshipping Popular?

Dropshipping has become popular for several reasons. Firstly, the startup cost is much lower than that of a traditional e-commerce business. Since the retailer doesn't have to purchase inventory upfront, there is no significant initial cost. Additionally, as the retailer doesn't have to manage inventory or shipping, there are no ongoing costs associated with these activities.

Secondly, dropshipping offers great flexibility. A retailer can add or remove products from their website at will without worrying about remaining inventory. This allows the retailer to easily test new products and adapt to changing market trends.

Finally, dropshipping allows the retailer to focus on what they do best: marketing and customer service. Instead of spending time managing inventory and shipments, the retailer can dedicate their time to attracting new customers and satisfying existing ones

❖ ❖ ❖

3. How to Start a Dropshipping Business?

Starting a dropshipping business involves several steps. The first step is to choose a product niche. It's important to select a niche that is both profitable and of personal interest. Once you've chosen a niche, you need to find one or more dropshippers who sell the products you want to offer. It's important to choose a reliable dropshipper with a good reputation. You can find dropshippers by searching online, using dropshipping directories, or by directly contacting manufacturers of the products you want to sell. Once you've found a dropshipper, you need to create your website. There are many e-commerce platforms that can help you build a professional website without requiring coding knowledge. You'll also need to choose a name for your business and create a logo. Next, you need to add your dropshipper's products to your website. You'll need to write compelling product descriptions and take high-quality product photos to attract customers. Finally, you need to promote your business. This may involve using social media, SEO, email marketing, and other online marketing strategies. In addition to these steps, if you are in France, you'll also need to establish a legal entity for your dropshipping business. The process of creating a company in France can vary depending on the type of company you choose.

Here are some general steps you'll need to follow:

a. Choose a Business Structure:
There are several types of business structures in France, including sole proprietorship, limited liability company (SARL), public limited company (SA), and simplified joint-stock company (SAS). Each type of structure has its own advantages and disadvantages, and the choice of structure will depend on your specific needs.

b. Register Your Business:
Once you've chosen a business structure, you'll need to register your business. This typically involves filling out a registration form, providing proof of a business address, and publishing a notice of company formation in a legal journal.

c. Obtain SIRET, SIREN, and APE Numbers:
These numbers are essential for registering your business in France. The SIREN number is a unique identifier for your business, while the SIRET number is an identifier for each establishment of your business. The APE code describes the primary activity of your business.

d. Open a Business Bank Account:
In France, it's generally necessary to open a separate bank account for your business. This helps separate your personal finances from your business finances, making it easier to manage your business and keep track of your accounts.

e. Register for VAT:
If your business reaches a certain level of turnover, you'll need to register for VAT.

f. Choose a Business Name:
You'll need to choose a unique business name and check that it's

not already in use. You can perform a simple free check or pay for a more detailed search. If you want exclusive use of the name you choose, you can register it for a fee.

g. Write a Business Plan:

A business plan is a document that describes your business, goals, marketing strategy, market analysis, and other important information about your business. It's typically required when you're starting a business.

h. Seek Legal and Accounting Advice:

It's advisable to consult with a lawyer and an accountant to help you navigate the business formation process. They can assist you in understanding the laws and regulations applicable to your business, prepare the necessary documents for registering your business, and manage your finances.

It's important to note that the process of creating a business in France can be complex and require a significant amount of time and effort. However, with proper planning and preparation, you can establish a successful dropshipping business in France.

4. The Benefits of Dropshipping

Dropshipping offers several advantages that make it appealing to entrepreneurs. Here are some of the key benefits of dropshipping:

a. Low Startup Cost:

Unlike a traditional retail business, you don't need to invest a lot of money to start a dropshipping business. You don't have to purchase inventory upfront, significantly reducing your startup costs.

b. Ease of Management:

With dropshipping, you don't have to worry about managing inventory or shipping products. Your dropshipper takes care of all of that for you.

c. Flexibility:

Dropshipping allows you to work from anywhere at any time. All you need is an internet connection.

d. Wide Selection of Products:

With dropshipping, you can sell a wide variety of products without having to stock them yourself. This gives you the opportunity to offer a broad selection of products to your customers.

e. Reduced Risk:

Since you don't have to buy inventory upfront, the financial risk associated with starting a dropshipping business is much lower than that of a traditional retail business.

However, it's important to note that dropshipping also comes with challenges. For example, you need to find a reliable dropshipper, deal with competition, and work with lower profit margins. Despite these challenges, dropshipping remains an excellent option for entrepreneurs looking to start a business.

5. Challenges of Dropshipping

While dropshipping offers many advantages, it also presents unique challenges that entrepreneurs must overcome to succeed. Here are some of the common challenges associated with dropshipping:

a. Finding New Products:

One of the toughest obstacles dropshippers face is the constant need to discover new products. The lifespan of most dropshipping products is about 5 to 6 months, which means that when a product becomes saturated, dropshippers need to find new products to sell.

b. Inventory Management:

Dropshipping businesses rely on third-party suppliers to store inventory and ship products, which can lead to issues with stock availability and shipping times.

c. Payment Issues:

Fulfilling orders from locations that do not accept certain payment processors, such as China, can also be problematic. This can result in issues with payment processors like PayPal, which may restrict funds flow by implementing a rolling reserve or hold on the account.

To overcome these challenges, dropshippers can implement various strategies. For example, they can conduct ongoing research to identify trending products and adjust their offerings to meet changing customer demands. They can also find local suppliers or warehouses and order in bulk to help address local storage and shipping issues. It's also crucial to follow certain best practices for running a successful dropshipping business. For instance, putting the customer first is essential, which means creating a user-friendly and navigable website that can increase conversion rates and generate more sales. Building strong relationships with suppliers is also crucial, as it can help dropshippers negotiate better prices and ensure that the quality of the products they sell is top-notch.

❖ ❖ ❖

6. Conclusion

Dropshipping is an e-commerce method that offers many benefits, including low startup costs, ease of management, and great flexibility. However, like any business, dropshipping also comes with challenges. It's important to understand these challenges and know how to overcome them to succeed in dropshipping. Additionally, dropshipping requires effective planning and strategy. Choosing a profitable product niche, finding a reliable dropshipper, and creating an attractive website are important steps. If you are in France, you'll also need to navigate the process of establishing a legal entity for your dropshipping business.

CHAPTER 2: UNDERSTANDING SHOPIFY

1. What is Shopify?

Shopify is a cloud-based e-commerce platform designed to help individuals and businesses create their own customized online stores. Launched in 2006, it's now one of the leading e-commerce platforms in the world, with over a million active merchants across approximately 175 countries.

The mission of Shopify is straightforward: to make commerce better for everyone. To achieve this, they've created a platform that enables anyone, from the solo entrepreneur to the large retailer, to start, manage, and grow their business.

Shopify is more than just an online storefront. It's a comprehensive e-commerce solution providing a range of services including payments, marketing, shipping, and customer relationship management tools.

a. Flexibility and Accessibility

One of the main advantages of Shopify is its flexibility. Whether you're selling physical products, digital products, services, memberships, paid events, rentals, or even courses and lessons, Shopify has the tools to assist you. You can customize your store's appearance with themes, add features through apps, and sell across various sales channels, including social media and online marketplaces.

Besides its flexibility, Shopify is also known for being user-friendly. Even if you lack experience in website design or coding, you can still set up an attractive, functional online store. Shopify offers an intuitive user interface and detailed guides to assist you at every step of the process.

b. Built-in Features

Shopify offers a variety of built-in features to help businesses efficiently manage their online stores. For instance, it has a unified dashboard where you can manage orders, track sales, and monitor your store's performance. It also provides tools to help in the creation, execution, and analysis of digital marketing campaigns.

Additionally, Shopify offers an integrated payment solution called Shopify Payments. This allows merchants to accept credit card payments directly on their store without needing a third-party merchant account. Shopify Payments is easy to set up and offers competitive rates.

c. Support and Resources

Shopify is renowned for its excellent customer support. They offer 24/7 assistance through live chat, email, and phone. Moreover, they have an extensive online knowledge base with guides, tutorials, and community forums to help merchants solve issues and learn how to use the platform.

Beyond customer support, Shopify also provides a variety of resources to help merchants succeed. For example, they have a Shopify Academy that offers free courses on e-commerce and entrepreneurship. They also have a blog featuring articles on a variety of topics.

Shopify continued to innovate and improve its services to help businesses grow and succeed. Here are some of the updates and key features that have been introduced:

i. *Powerful Global Infrastructure*

Shopify has significantly expanded its global infrastructure, enabling sites to load quickly regardless of where the customers are located. With 270 points of presence worldwide and new locations being rolled out, sites on Shopify respond twice as fast.

ii. *New One-Page Checkout*

Shopify has introduced an entirely new one-page checkout, inspired by Shop Pay's proven conversion rate. This new checkout is faster, converts better, and exactly meets customers' expectations. Additionally, Shopify introduced a drag-and-drop checkout editor that enables merchants to easily customize their checkout's appearance.

iii. *Shop Promise*

To help build customer trust, Shopify has introduced the "Shop Promise." By installing the Shop channel and adding the Shop Promise badge and delivery dates to their store, merchants can communicate fast and reliable delivery to their customers. If delivery dates are missed, customers receive limited compensation.

iv. *Shop Connect*

Shopify also introduced a feature that allows high-intent Shop users to log in before reaching the checkout with their Shop credentials, including saved passkeys. This allows customers to quickly go through a one-click checkout using Shop Pay, reducing bounce rates and increasing conversions.

v. *Image Optimization and Focal Points*

To improve store speed and increase conversion rates, Shopify optimizes images for the highest quality and the lowest file size. Merchants can now select the focal point on images so that their products appear in the foreground.

vi.   AI-Generated Storefront Content

To help merchants overcome writer's block, Shopify has introduced a feature that automatically generates product descriptions. Merchants can input keywords or features, and the system generates a description. This results in compelling, tone-specific descriptions that convert better.

These improvements and features demonstrate how Shopify continually strives to enhance the experience for merchants and their customers. Whether you're a solo entrepreneur just starting out or an established business looking to expand, Shopify has the tools to help you succeed.

2.   How Does Shopify Work?

Shopify is a comprehensive e-commerce platform that allows you to start, grow, and manage a business. It consolidates all your commerce activities into a single platform. With Shopify, merchants can build and customize an online store and sell across various platforms, including web, mobile, in-person at physical locations, and through multiple channels—from social media to online marketplaces.

Shopify is entirely cloud-based and hosted, meaning you can access it from any compatible, connected device. Shopify takes care of software updates and server maintenance for you. This provides you the flexibility to access and manage your business from anywhere with an internet connection.

You can think of Shopify's product as layers that you can select to build the right stack for your business:

a. Layer 1: Shopify's Core Product

This is what you get as soon as you purchase any Shopify plan. It includes everything you need to turn your idea into a business and start selling. From templates for your store's appearance to tools for selling across multiple online and in-person locations, integrated payment processing, the most high-converting checkout on the internet, and SEO and marketing tools—this all comes as part of Shopify's core product. This is the foundation upon which our other products and apps are built.

b. Layer 2: Shopify's Additional Products and Services

Every independent business is unique, and as businesses grow, their needs evolve accordingly. That's why Shopify offers its customers powerful upgrades to help them expand their business on our platform. From easier access to capital to accelerated payment options, these products and services are exclusive to Shopify clients and are designed to give independent business owners a competitive edge.

c. Layer 3: Apps Built by Trusted Partners

Shopify's app store boasts thousands of apps and features built by third-party developers to customize your store without ever touching code. You'll find the most advanced tools for growing your business in the app store, whether it's the latest SMS app or advertising tools for the hottest new social media networks.

In summary, Shopify is designed to scale with you, regardless of your technical maturity, growth, size, complexity, or location. You'll never have limited access to technology and features to build your business, and you'll never outgrow Shopify as your needs change, evolve, or expand.

3. The Advantages of Shopify

Shopify is an e-commerce platform that offers numerous benefits for businesses, especially those selling a large number of physical products. Here are some of the key advantages of using Shopify:

a. User-Friendly Interface

Shopify is renowned for its user-friendly interface. It doesn't require any technical skills to use. You don't need to hire a developer; you can set up a website in less than 48 hours. It's a platform that has created more millionaires than any other tool I've ever seen, according to Paul Waddy, an e-commerce expert and author of "Shopify for Dummies."

b. Flexible Plans and Pricing

Shopify offers a range of pricing plans to cater to businesses of different sizes. Whether you're a small startup or a large enterprise handling high sales volume, Shopify has a plan that can meet your needs. Moreover, each plan comes with a set of features that can help your business grow.

c. Advanced Inventory and Order Management

Shopify provides advanced inventory and order management tools. Sellers can track and manage incoming and committed stocks, as well as move stocks between stores and warehouses. The Shopify dashboard displays customer orders that have already been placed. They can sort orders based on fulfillment method or delivery location and make changes if needed before orders are shipped.

d. Integrations with Social Media and Online Marketplaces

Shopify allows sellers to list their products on Facebook, Instagram, YouTube, TikTok, Google, and Walmart Marketplace. They can choose the platforms that best align with their brand and audience, then manage all their orders from the same dashboard that powers the rest of their Shopify store.

e. Reduced Shipping Rates

Shopify sellers have access to special shipping rates with carriers including USPS, UPS, DHL Express, and Canada Post. Shopify also includes shipping label printing and up to $200 in parcel insurance, which can protect shipments against damage and theft.

f. Shopify Payments

Shopify Payments is Shopify's integrated payment processing solution. It's easy to set up and allows businesses to accept online payments without having to configure a third-party payment processor. Shopify Payments offers competitive rates and is included in all Shopify plans.

g. Customer Support

Shopify offers 24/7 customer support via live chat, email, and phone. Users also have access to an extensive online knowledge base.

h. Social Media Support

Shopify has an impressive presence on all social media platforms. With nearly four million likes on Facebook, over 3,000 posts on Instagram, and more than 325,000 followers on Twitter, Shopify is undoubtedly popular. On Facebook, once you navigate to the Shopify page, you can initiate a live chat by clicking the "Message" button. While not as quick or efficient as going directly through the live chat tool on the Shopify website, it can be helpful if you're a regular Facebook user. On Twitter, you can tweet Shopify with your inquiry. Of course, this has the advantage of making your customer support request public, which means Shopify should care enough about its reputation to respond if it hasn't already. On Instagram, you can tag Shopify in posts or stories and summarize your issue or support request in the image caption.

i. Webinars and Community Events

Shopify offers webinars and community events to help users learn more about using the platform. Webinars are free and take place every day. They cover a variety of topics, from migrating from Etsy to Shopify to setting up Google Shopping with Shopify. Community events are in-person gatherings where you can learn from Shopify and your peers. Whether it's a seminar to help you get started with Shopify online in Miami or some festive e-commerce tips in Manila, there's something for everyone, everywhere.

j. Shopify's YouTube Channel

Shopify's YouTube channel is another valuable resource for users. It's filled with video guides covering everything from signing up for a free trial to selecting a payment provider. The 333,000 subscribers attest to its value.

k. Shopify App Store

Shopify's App Store is another major advantage of the platform. It offers a multitude of apps that can be integrated into your store to enhance its functionality. Whether you need an app to manage your inventory, automate your email marketing, or improve your store's SEO, you're likely to find it in the Shopify App Store.

l. Security

Shopify is a highly secure platform. It complies with PCI DSS level 1 standard, meaning it adheres to the highest standards of credit card data security. Moreover, all Shopify stores are automatically equipped with a free SSL certificate to secure your customers' information.

m. Shopify POS

Shopify POS (Point of Sale) is an application that allows you to sell products in person while keeping all your sales and inventory data synchronized. Here are some of the benefits of Shopify POS:

i. Order and Product Management

Shopify POS Lite, available for free with the entry-level Shopify plan, offers order and product management features. This means you can track customer orders and manage your inventory directly from the app.

ii. Staff Permissions and Roles

With the Shopify plan, which costs $79 per month with annual billing, you get additional features like staff permissions and roles. This is particularly useful for businesses with multiple people managing their site.

iii. Omnichannel Selling

The Shopify plan also offers omnichannel selling, allowing you to sell your products through a variety of sales channels while keeping all your data synchronized.

iv. In-Store Inventory Management and Analysis

For those with physical retail space, the Shopify plan offers in-store inventory management and analysis features.

v. User-Friendly Interface

Shopify POS is known for its user-friendly interface, making it easy to use and navigate. However, it offers limited customization options beyond the basics.

vi. Security

Security is a priority for Shopify POS, offering industry-standard SSL encryption to ensure that data transmitted between devices and servers is secure. Additionally, it has built-in fraud prevention tools to detect and prevent fraudulent activity.

vii.   PCI Compliance

Shopify POS is PCI DSS compliant and undergoes regular audits to ensure ongoing compliance.

viii.   Customer Service and Support

Shopify offers customer support through a bot that prequalifies whether you can be directly connected to a human to answer your questions. There are also several self-help options, including an FAQ, the Shopify Help Center, and the Shopify community.

n.   Shopify Academy

Shopify Academy is a free online learning platform that offers courses on a variety of e-commerce-related topics. Whether you're a beginner looking to learn the basics of e-commerce or an experienced seller looking to refine your skills, Shopify Academy has something for you.

o.   Shopify Experts

Shopify Experts is a directory of independent professionals and agencies that can help businesses develop and improve their Shopify store. Whether you need assistance with store design, development, marketing, SEO, photography, or content writing, you can find a Shopify expert to assist you. Here are some of the advantages of using Shopify Experts:

i.   Specialized Expertise

Shopify Experts have in-depth knowledge of the Shopify platform and specialize in different areas. Whether you need help with store design, development, marketing, SEO, photography, or content writing, you can find a Shopify expert to assist you.

ii. Extensive Network

Shopify Experts have built extensive networks. They are connected to individuals, businesses, and organizations worldwide that offer specialized services such as marketing, web design, content creation, analytics, and more. This gives them access to a variety of services to help their clients succeed.

iii. Deep Understanding of Shopify

Thanks to their extensive network, Shopify Experts have a deep understanding of the unique challenges and opportunities of the Shopify platform. They can develop customized solutions for their clients.

iv. Access to Resources

Shopify Experts have access to a multitude of resources to help their clients succeed. This is also the main reason why many online sellers are willing to invest money in hiring a suitable Shopify Expert for their store.

To hire a Shopify Expert, it is recommended to define your business requirements, conduct a quick search for certified Shopify Experts, check their portfolios and reviews, discuss pricing and job requirements, conduct an interview, and finally, sign a contract with the expert.

In summary, Shopify offers a multitude of advantages that make it an attractive e-commerce platform for businesses of all sizes. Whether you're a newcomer to e-commerce or an experienced seller, Shopify has something to offer to help you succeed in your online business.

4. How to Get Started with Shopify for Dropshipping

a. Signing up on Shopify

The first step to get started with Shopify is to sign up on their platform. You can do this by visiting their website and clicking on the "Get Started" button. You'll need to provide some basic information like your email address, a password, and the name of your store. It's important to note that your store's name must be unique, so if the name you've chosen is already taken, you'll need to choose another one.

b. Setting up your store

Once you've created your account, you'll be directed to your store's dashboard. Here, you can start setting up your store by adding products, customizing your store's design, configuring your payment and shipping settings, and more.

c. Adding products

Adding products to your Shopify store is a straightforward process. You can do it by going to the "Products" section of your dashboard and clicking on "Add a product." You'll need to provide information about the product, such as its name, price, description, and you can also add product images.

d. Customizing your store's design

Shopify offers a variety of themes that you can use to customize your store's design. You can access these themes by going to the "Themes" section of your dashboard. You can choose from the free themes offered by Shopify, or you can opt to purchase a premium theme.

e. Configuring payment and shipping settings

To receive payments from your customers and organize the shipping of your products, you'll need to configure your payment and shipping settings. You can do this by going to the "Settings" section of your dashboard and selecting "Payments" and "Shipping."

f. Launching your store

Once you've set up your store and you're ready to start selling, you can launch your store by going to the "Settings" section of your dashboard and selecting "Preferences." Here, you can remove the password from your store, allowing customers to visit and make purchases in your store.

g. Managing your store

After launching your store, you'll need to manage it by adding new products, processing customer orders, responding to customer inquiries, and more. Shopify provides a variety of tools to help you manage your store, including a dashboard to track your sales and performance, a section to manage your products and orders, and a section to communicate with your customers.

h. Using Shopify for Dropshipping

Shopify is an excellent platform for dropshipping. With Shopify, you can easily add dropshipping products from suppliers to your store, and when these products are sold, the supplier takes care of shipping. Here's how you can use Shopify for dropshipping:

  i. *Install the Oberlo dropshipping app*

Shopify has developed its own dropshipping app, Oberlo, to ensure seamless integration with the platform. You can go to the Shopify App Store and install Oberlo to connect your Shopify store to thousands of suppliers on AliExpress.

> ii. *Sync Shopify and Oberlo with your AliExpress account*

This unlocks useful features like automatic order quantity updates directly from suppliers.

> iii. *Browse products on Oberlo and import product data you like directly into your Shopify store*

This only takes a few clicks as the process is entirely automated. You can sort products by order quantity to know which ones sell best on dropshipping sites.

> iv. *Edit product descriptions, images, and variant details before importing them*

This is an optional but recommended step to customize your product catalog.

> v. *Fulfill orders with Oberlo*

After a customer has purchased a product in your Shopify store, you can use Oberlo to fulfill the order. The process is entirely automated and takes just a few clicks.

> vi. *Send the order to the dropshipping supplier*

Make sure you're logged into your AliExpress account and have installed the Oberlo Chrome extension. Verify that all order details are correct, especially the shipping method, and send the order to the dropshipper.

> vii. *Handle returns and refunds*

Even though you have nothing to do with shipping and product management in your store, you're responsible for addressing customer complaints about issues you don't control, such as incomplete orders, wrong color, or damaged packaging.

viii.   Avoid costly mistakes

If you're new to dropshipping with Shopify, there can be a learning curve. A silly mistake like paying for Google ads when the product was out of stock or inserting the wrong link in Facebook ads can cost you money.

ix.   Test the market

Dropshipping allows you to test new products or markets without committing too much. For example, you can add new products to your store and see how they sell before deciding to invest more resources in those products.

x.   Find dropshipping suppliers other than AliExpress

If you want to start dropshipping with suppliers other than AliExpress, you can use dropshipping supplier directories. They are huge databases of wholesalers, suppliers, and manufacturers. Here are some methods to find these suppliers:

• **Call the manufacturer:** If you know which product you want to dropship, call the manufacturer and ask for a list of their dropshipping wholesalers. You can then contact these wholesalers to see if they do dropshipping and inquire about setting up an account.

• **Google search:** Wholesalers are usually bad at marketing and promotion, and they definitely won't be at the top of search results for "wholesale suppliers for product X." This means you'll likely have to dig through a lot of search results - possibly hundreds - to find the wholesaler's website.

• **Order from competitors:** If you're struggling to locate product suppliers for dropshipping, you can always use the "order from competitors" trick. Here's how it works: find a competitor you think is dropshipping and place a small order with that company. When you receive the package, look up the return address to find out who the original shipper was. In some cases, it may be a supplier you can contact.

• **Attend a trade show:** A trade show allows you to connect with all the major manufacturers and wholesalers in a niche. It's a great way to make contacts and research your products and suppliers, all in one place.

• **Test the market:** Dropshipping allows you to test new products or markets without committing too much. For example, you can add new products to your store and see how they sell before deciding to invest more resources in those products.

• **Use dropshipping supplier directories:** Some of the best dropshipping suppliers are listed in dropshipping supplier directories. These directories are massive databases of wholesalers, suppliers, and manufacturers. Some of the most popular ones include AliExpress, Alibaba, SaleHoo, Worldwide Brands, Doba, Sunrise Wholesale, Wholesale2B, MegaGoods, Modalyst, Wholesale Central, Spocket, CJDropshipping, and Crov.

In summary, Shopify is a powerful platform that offers a multitude of tools to assist in the creation and management of an online store. Whether you're a beginner entrepreneur or an experienced seller, Shopify has something to offer everyone.

5. Shopify and Dropshipping

Dropshipping is a business model that allows entrepreneurs to sell products manufactured, stored, and shipped by third-party suppliers from their own online stores. Shopify is an e-commerce platform that greatly facilitates dropshipping through its many features and integrations.

a. How Does Dropshipping with Shopify Work?

With Shopify, dropshipping is streamlined through a variety of apps that connect directly to suppliers. These apps automate the shipping process by manufacturing, storing, and shipping products on your behalf. Popular dropshipping apps on Shopify include Spocket, DSers, and Modalyst.

Spocket includes products from dropshipping suppliers in the US, Canada, Europe, Australia, Brazil, and more. The app also syncs with AliExpress, allowing users to import products directly into their Shopify stores.

DSers allows merchants to search, import, and edit product data from suppliers on AliExpress. One notable feature is the ability to compare AliExpress dropshippers selling the same products, allowing merchants to find the best price for their products.

Modalyst, like the other options, also syncs with AliExpress, making it easy to import products directly into the Shopify store. Modalyst also offers curated lists of independent brands as well as higher-end brands like Calvin Klein and Dolce & Gabbana.

CHAPTER 3: HOW TO CREATE A SHOPIFY STORE

Shopify is an e-commerce platform that allows anyone to create an online store and sell products. Whether you sell online, on social media, in a physical store, or from the trunk of your car, Shopify has a solution for you. Here's how you can create your own Shopify store.

◆ ◆ ◆

1. Step 1: Sign up for Shopify

The first step in creating a Shopify store is to sign up for Shopify. This step, although simple on the surface, is crucial for the success of your business. It lays the foundation for your online store and allows you to start building your online presence.

a. Visit the Shopify website

To begin, you need to visit the Shopify website. You can do this by opening your web browser and typing "www.shopify.com" in the address bar. Once you're on the Shopify website, you'll see a homepage with various options. You can learn more about

Shopify's features, read testimonials from satisfied customers, or even check out their blog for e-commerce tips. However, for now, your goal is to create a store, so look for the "Get Started" or "Free Trial" button and click on it.

b. Create an account

After clicking the "Get Started" button, you'll be directed to a page where you can create an account. Creating an account is a simple process that should only take a few minutes. You'll need to provide a valid email address, create a password, and give your store a name.

When choosing an email address, make sure to use one you check regularly. Shopify will use this address to send you important information about your store, such as sales notifications, product updates, and tips to improve your store.

Choosing a strong and secure password is also crucial. Your password protects your store from unauthorized access, so it should be strong and secure. Try using a combination of letters, numbers, and symbols to make your password harder to guess.

Finally, you'll need to give your store a name. The name of your store is important because it represents your brand and gives customers a first impression of your business. Try to choose a name that is unique, easy to remember, and gives an idea of what you sell.

c. Completing the registration

Once you've filled in this information, you can click "Create Your Store." Shopify will then process your information and create your store. This process may take a few minutes, so please be patient.

While you wait, you can start thinking about the next step in creating your Shopify store: configuring your store. You'll need to choose a theme for your store, add products, and configure your payment and shipping settings. Each of these steps is crucial to the success of your store, so take the time to consider your options and plan accordingly.

In conclusion, signing up for Shopify is a simple but important step in creating your online store. By taking the time to choose an appropriate email address, a secure password, and a unique store name, you can lay the foundation for a successful online store.

2. Step 2: Setting up Your Store

After creating your Shopify account and naming your store, the next step is to set up your store. This step is essential to ensure the smooth operation of your store and to provide your customers with a pleasant and hassle-free shopping experience. Setting up your store includes several sub-steps, such as customizing your store, adding products, and configuring your settings.

a. Accessing your store's dashboard

Once you've created your store, you'll be directed to your store's dashboard. The dashboard is where you'll manage all aspects of your store, from adding products to monitoring sales. It's designed intuitively, making it easy to navigate and manage your store.

On the dashboard, you'll see several options in the left

menu, including "Home," "Orders," "Products," "Customers," "Analytics," "Marketing," "Discounts," and "Apps." Each option allows you to manage a different aspect of your store.

b. Customizing your store

Customizing your store is an important step in creating a strong brand identity and attracting and retaining customers. Shopify offers a variety of customization options that allow you to give your store the look and feel you desire.

To start customizing your store, click on "Themes" in the left menu of your dashboard. Here, you can choose a theme for your store, customize that theme, and preview your store.

Choosing a theme is a significant decision because it determines the appearance of your store. Shopify offers a variety of free and paid themes that you can use. Each theme has a different style and design, so take the time to browse the available themes and choose the one that best suits your brand and products.

Once you've chosen a theme, you can customize it to match your brand. You can change colors, fonts, images, and more. Take the time to customize every aspect of your theme to create a store that reflects your brand and appeals to your customers.

c. Adding products to your store

Adding products to your store is another crucial step in setting up your store. Without products, you have nothing to sell, and without something to sell, you can't do e-commerce.

To add products to your store, click on "Products" in the left menu of your dashboard. Here, you can add products, create product collections, and manage your inventory.

When adding a product, you'll need to provide information about the product, such as the title, description, price, and images. Make sure to provide accurate and detailed information to help your customers understand what they're purchasing.

d. Configuring your settings

Configuring your settings is the final step in setting up your store. Your settings include things like your billing information, payment settings, shipping settings, and more.

To access your settings, click on "Settings" in the left menu of your dashboard. Here, you'll see several options, including "General," "Payments," "Shipping," "Taxes," "Notifications," "Billing," "Files," "Sales Channels," "Plan and Permissions," "Store languages," "Checkout," "Legal," "Gift cards," "Google Shopping," "Metafields," and "Shipping and delivery."

Each option allows you to configure a different aspect of your store. For example, the "General" settings allow you to edit basic information about your store, such as your email address, currency, and time zone. The "Payments" settings allow you to choose how you accept payments from your customers. The "Shipping" settings allow you to configure your shipping options and calculate shipping fees.

It's important to take the time to review each option and configure your settings based on your needs and those of your customers. Properly configuring your settings can improve your customers' shopping experience and make managing your store easier.

e. Conclusion

Setting up your Shopify store is a crucial step in creating your online store. By taking the time to customize your store, add products, and configure your settings, you can create a store that reflects your brand, attracts customers, and makes managing your business easier.

However, setting up your store is just the beginning. Once your store is configured, you'll need to work on promoting your store, engaging your customers, and optimizing your store to increase sales and customer satisfaction. But with a well-configured store, you've already taken a big step toward the success of your e-commerce business.

◆ ◆ ◆

3. Step 3: Adding Products

Adding products to your Shopify store is an essential step in bringing your online store to life. This is where you'll start building your product catalog, defining your offerings, and showing your customers what you have to offer. In the context of dropshipping, this step also involves selecting products from third-party suppliers and adding them to your store. Shopify makes this process easier with a variety of apps that can help automate the dropshipping process.

a. Accessing the "Products" section of your dashboard

To begin adding products to your Shopify store, you'll need to access the "Products" section of your dashboard. To do this, log in to your Shopify account and click on "Products" in the left menu of your dashboard. This will take you to a page where you can see all the products you've already added to your store and where you can add new products.

b. Adding a product

To add a product, click the "Add a product" button on the

Products page. This will take you to a new page where you can enter information about the product you're adding.

When adding a product, you'll need to provide several pieces of information, including the product's title, description, images, price, and more. Each piece of information you provide helps inform your customers about the product and assists them in making a purchasing decision.

The product's title is what your customers will see when they browse your store. It should be clear and descriptive while being concise enough for easy readability.

The product description is where you can provide more details about the product. You can include information about the product's features, uses, benefits, and any other details that might be helpful to your customers. Make sure to be as detailed as possible in your product descriptions to help your customers understand what they're buying.

Product images are also crucial. They allow your customers to see what the product looks like and get an idea of what to expect if they purchase the product. Try to include multiple images that show the product from different angles and in different usage contexts.

The price of the product is, of course, one of the most important factors that influence your customers' purchasing decisions. Make sure to set a price that reflects the value of the product while considering your costs and pricing strategy.

c. Dropshipping and Shopify apps

In the context of dropshipping, adding products to your store may involve a few additional steps. Instead of stocking the products yourself, you'll work with a third-party supplier who will store and ship the products on your behalf. This means you'll need to choose products to sell from your supplier's catalog.

Shopify makes dropshipping easier through various apps that can help automate the process. Apps like Oberlo, Spocket, and Modalyst can assist you in finding dropshipping suppliers, importing products into your Shopify store, and automating the shipping process.

For example, Oberlo is a popular app that allows you to find products to sell from various dropshipping suppliers. You can browse their product catalog, choose the products you want to sell, and import them directly into your Shopify store. When a customer purchases a product, the order is automatically sent to the supplier for shipping.

Spocket and Modalyst work similarly but offer different product catalogs and may have additional features. For instance, Spocket focuses on suppliers based in the United States and Europe, while Modalyst offers a range of products from independent brands.

Using these apps can greatly simplify the dropshipping process and allow you to manage your store more efficiently. However, it's important to do your research and choose products and suppliers that align with your brand and your customers.

d. Managing inventory

As part of setting up your products, you'll also need to manage your inventory. Shopify makes inventory management easy by allowing you to track the quantity of each product you have in stock. If you're dropshipping, your supplier will handle inventory, but you still need to monitor stock levels to avoid selling products that are out of stock.

To manage your inventory, go to the "Products" page in your Shopify dashboard and click on the product you want to manage. Here, you can set the number of available products, enable inventory tracking, and configure notifications to be alerted when inventory is low.

e. Conclusion

Adding products to your Shopify store is a crucial step in bringing your online store to life. Whether you're selling your own products or dropshipping, it's important to choose quality products, provide detailed and accurate product information, and efficiently manage your inventory. With Shopify's tools and features, you can easily add products to your store and start selling.

4. Step 4: Setting up Payment and Shipping Settings

After adding products to your Shopify store, the next step is to configure your payment and shipping settings. These settings are essential to ensure a smooth shopping experience for your customers and to ensure that you receive payments efficiently and securely.

a. Configuring Payment Settings

The first part of this step is to configure your payment settings. Shopify offers a variety of payment options that you can offer to your customers, including credit cards, PayPal, Apple Pay, and more.

To configure your payment settings, go to your Shopify store's dashboard and click on "Settings," then select "Payments." Here, you'll see a list of different payment providers you can use.

Shopify Payments is Shopify's default payment provider and is a popular choice for many store owners. It offers seamless integration with your Shopify store, accepts a variety of payment methods, and offers competitive rates. To activate Shopify Payments, click "Enable" next to Shopify Payments and follow the instructions to set up your account.

If you prefer to use another payment provider or if you want to offer multiple payment options to your customers, you can also enable other payment providers. Simply click "Choose an alternative payment provider" and select the payment provider you want to use.

It's important to note that different payment providers may have different fees, payment options, and requirements for using their services. Be sure to do your research and choose the payment provider that best fits your needs and those of your customers.

b. Configuring Shipping Settings

The second part of this step is to configure your shipping settings. These settings determine how and where you ship your products, how much you charge for shipping, and what shipping options you offer to your customers.

To configure your shipping settings, go to your Shopify store's dashboard and click on "Settings," then select "Shipping." Here, you'll see several options for configuring your shipping settings.

The first thing you'll need to do is set up your shipping zones. Shipping zones are the geographical regions where you're willing to ship your products. For each shipping zone, you can set specific shipping rates and shipping methods.

To add a shipping zone, click "Add shipping zone," give your zone a name, and select the countries or regions that are part of that zone. Once you've added the countries or regions, you can set your shipping rates for that zone.

Shipping rates are the fees you charge your customers for shipping their products. You can set fixed shipping rates, weight-based rates, or price-based rates. You can also offer free shipping, which can be a powerful incentive for customers.

In addition to setting your shipping rates, you can also choose the shipping methods you offer. For example, you can offer standard shipping, express shipping, or same-day shipping. Each shipping method can have different shipping rates, so be sure to set rates for each method you offer.

If you're dropshipping, you'll also need to consider your supplier's shipping settings. Some suppliers may offer free shipping, while others may charge shipping fees. Make sure to understand your supplier's shipping policies and take them into account when configuring your own shipping settings.

c. Conclusion

Configuring payment and shipping settings is a crucial step to ensure a smooth shopping experience for your customers and to ensure that you receive payments efficiently and securely. By taking the time to configure these settings correctly, you can offer your customers a variety of payment and shipping options, which can help increase sales and customer satisfaction.

5. Step 5: Choosing and Customizing a Theme for Your Store

The appearance of your online store plays a crucial role in your customers' shopping experience. An attractive and professional design can help attract customers, enhance your brand's credibility, and increase conversions. Shopify offers a variety of themes that you can use for your store, each offering a unique range of styles, features, and customization.

a. Selecting a Shopify Theme

To choose a theme for your Shopify store, start by navigating to the "Themes" section of your Shopify dashboard. You can access it by clicking on "Themes" in the left menu of your dashboard.

Once you're in the "Themes" section, you'll see a variety of free and paid themes to choose from. Free themes are a great option if you're just starting out or have a limited budget. They provide a clean and professional design that can be sufficient for many stores.

Paid themes, on the other hand, generally offer more features and customization options. They may include additional features like slideshows, featured product sections, social media integrations, and more. If you have a larger budget and want a more unique design for your store, a paid theme can be a good investment.

When choosing a theme, consider the look and feel you want for your store. Think about your brand, products, and target audience. For example, if you're selling luxury products, you may want a theme that reflects that upscale image. If you're selling fun and colorful products, a more playful and vibrant theme might be more suitable.

b. Customizing Your Theme

Once you've selected a theme, you can customize it to match your brand and products. To do this, click on "Customize" next to the theme you've chosen. This will take you to the Shopify theme editor, where you can edit colors, fonts, images, layouts, and more.

The Shopify theme editor is designed to be user-friendly, even if you don't have experience in design or coding. It uses a drag-and-drop system that allows you to easily add, remove, and rearrange sections of your store. You can also click on any section to edit its settings, such as changing a background image or modifying text.

When customizing your theme, keep the user experience in mind. Ensure that your store is easy to navigate, your products are showcased, and your brand is clearly represented. Use high-quality images, clear and detailed product descriptions, and a color palette that aligns with your brand.

c. Conclusion

Choosing and customizing a theme for your Shopify store is an important step in creating an attractive and effective online store. By selecting a theme that matches your brand and products and customizing it to meet your customers' needs, you can create a store that attracts customers, enhances your brand's credibility, and increases conversions.

6. Step 6: Optimizing Your Store for SEO

Search engine optimization (SEO) is a crucial element in increasing the visibility of your Shopify store. By optimizing your store for SEO, you increase the chances of your store appearing in search engine results like Google, which can lead to more traffic to your store and ultimately more sales. Here are some key steps to optimize your Shopify store for SEO.

a. Understanding SEO

Before you begin optimizing your store, it's important to understand what SEO is and why it's important. SEO, or search engine optimization, is the process of improving your website to increase its visibility in organic search engine results. The more visible your site is in search results, the more likely you are to attract visitors to your site. SEO is important because it can help increase traffic to your site, which can lead to increased sales.

b. Optimizing Product Titles, Descriptions, and Image Alt Tags

One of the first steps in optimizing your store for SEO is to ensure that your product titles, descriptions, and image alt tags contain relevant keywords that your customers might use to find your products. These elements are important because they help search engines understand what your site is about and when it should appear in search results.

To optimize your product titles, try to include relevant keywords that describe your product and are likely to be used by your customers when searching for similar products. For example, if you're selling running shoes, you could include keywords like "running shoes," "sports shoes," or "women's running shoes" in your product titles.

Similarly, your product descriptions should be detailed and contain relevant keywords. However, it's important to ensure that your product descriptions are written for humans, not search engines. This means they should be informative, engaging, and helpful to your customers while still containing relevant keywords.

Finally, don't forget to optimize your image alt tags. Image alt tags are textual descriptions of your images that help search engines understand what your images represent. They are also useful for users who may not be able to see your images for any reason, such as those using screen readers. To optimize your image alt tags, try to include relevant keywords that describe the image and the product it represents.

c. Optimizing Your Site Structure

The structure of your site, or how your pages are organized and linked together, is another important element of search engine optimization. A good site structure can help search engines understand your site and determine which content is most important. It can also help your visitors navigate your site and find what they're looking for, which can lead to a better user experience and increased sales.

To optimize your site structure, try to keep your site as simple and organized as possible. This means having a clear hierarchy of pages, with main pages linking to relevant sub-pages. For example, you might have a main page for "Shoes" that links to sub-pages for "Running Shoes," "Walking Shoes," and "Hiking Shoes."

It's also important to use internal links to connect your pages. Internal links are links that go from one page on your site to another page on your site. They help search engines understand the relationship between your pages and can help improve your site's ranking in search results.

d. Optimizing Your Site Speed

Site speed is another important factor for SEO. Search engines like Google take into account the speed of your site when determining where to place your site in search results. Additionally, a slow site can frustrate your visitors and lead them to leave your site, which can result in decreased sales.

To optimize your site speed, you can use tools like Google PageSpeed Insights or GTmetrix to analyze your site's speed and receive recommendations on how to improve it. This can include things like compressing your images, reducing the number of plugins or apps you use, and optimizing your code.

e. Using SEO Analytics

Finally, it's important to use SEO analytics to track your site's performance and identify areas that may need improvement. Shopify offers a variety of SEO analytics tools that you can use to track your site's performance, including Google Analytics, Google Search Console, and their own integrated SEO analytics tool.

These tools can help you understand how visitors interact with your site, what keywords they use to find your site, and which pages on your site are most popular. You can use this information to improve your site and your SEO strategy.

In conclusion, optimizing your Shopify store for SEO is an important process that can help increase your store's visibility, attract more visitors, and increase sales. By understanding SEO, optimizing your product titles, descriptions, and image alt tags, optimizing your site structure, improving site speed, and using SEO analytics, you can create a Shopify store that is SEO-optimized and ready for success.

7. Step 7: Setting Up Google Analytics and Facebook Pixel

Setting up Google Analytics and Facebook Pixel is a crucial step in tracking your store's performance and understanding your customers' behavior. These tools allow you to gather valuable data on user interactions with your site, which can help you optimize your store and improve your marketing efforts.

a. Part 1: Setting Up Google Analytics

Google Analytics is a free service that allows you to track your website's traffic and understand how visitors interact with your store. It provides access to a wealth of data, including the number of visitors to your site, the time they spend on your site, the pages they visit, and more.

To set up Google Analytics on Shopify, you first need to create a Google Analytics account. Once you've created your account, you'll receive a Google Analytics tracking ID, which you'll need to add to your Shopify store. Here are the steps to set up Google Analytics on Shopify:

i. *Create a Google Analytics account if you don't already have one. You can do this by visiting the Google Analytics website and following the instructions to create a new account.*

ii. *Once you've created your account, you'll receive a Google Analytics tracking ID. This ID is unique to your account and is*

necessary to connect your Shopify store to Google Analytics.
- *iii.   Log in to your Shopify account and go to your store's dashboard.*
- *iv.   Click on "Settings" in the left menu, then "Preferences."*
- *v.   Scroll down to the "Google Analytics" section and paste your Google Analytics tracking ID into the provided field.*
- *vi.   Click "Save" to save your changes.*

Once you've added your Google Analytics tracking ID to your Shopify store, Google Analytics will begin tracking your site's traffic. You can view your Google Analytics data by logging into your Google Analytics account and navigating to your Google Analytics dashboard.

b.   Part 2: Setting Up Facebook Pixel

Facebook Pixel is a tracking tool that allows you to measure the effectiveness of your Facebook ads by tracking the actions users take on your site. With Facebook Pixel, you can track conversions, create custom audiences for your ads, and gain valuable insights into how users interact with your site after seeing your Facebook ads.

To set up Facebook Pixel on Shopify, you first need to create a Facebook Pixel. Once you've created your pixel, you'll receive a pixel ID that you'll need to add to your Shopify store. Here are the steps to set up Facebook Pixel on Shopify:

- *i.   Create a Facebook Pixel if you don't already have one. You can do this by visiting the Facebook Ads Manager and following the instructions to create a new pixel.*
- *ii.   Once you've created your pixel, you'll receive a pixel ID. This ID is unique to your pixel and is necessary to connect your Shopify store to Facebook Pixel.*
- *iii.   Log in to your Shopify account and go to your store's dashboard.*

After creating your Facebook Pixel, you need to install it on your website. To do this, follow these steps:

iv. *Log in to your Shopify account and go to your store's dashboard.*
v. *Click on "Settings" in the left menu, then "Preferences."*
vi. *Scroll down to the "Facebook Pixel" section and paste your pixel ID into the provided field.*
vii. *Click "Save" to save your changes.*

Once you've added your pixel ID to your Shopify store, Facebook Pixel will start tracking user actions on your site. You can view your Facebook Pixel data by logging into your Facebook account and navigating to your Facebook Pixel dashboard.

It's important to note that Facebook Pixel and Google Analytics work together. While Google Analytics provides detailed information about user behavior on your site, Facebook Pixel helps you understand how users interact with your Facebook ads. By using these two tools in tandem, you can get a comprehensive view of your store's effectiveness and your marketing efforts.

c. Part 3: Using Google Analytics and Facebook Pixel to Improve Your Store

Once you've set up Google Analytics and Facebook Pixel, you can start using the data they provide to improve your store. Here are some ways you can use these tools:

i. *Understanding Your Customers:*

Google Analytics and Facebook Pixel provide valuable information about your customers, including their location, age, gender, devices they use to access your site, and more. You can use this information to understand who your customers are and what they're looking for.

ii. *Tracking Store Performance:*

These tools allow you to track various metrics, including the number of visitors to your site, the time they spend on your site, the pages they visit, the number of conversions you get, and more. You can use this information to understand how your store is performing and where you can make improvements.

iii. *Optimizing Your Marketing Efforts:*

Google Analytics and Facebook Pixel allow you to track the effectiveness of your marketing efforts. You can see which ads generate the most traffic and conversions, which marketing channels are most effective, and more. You can use this information to optimize your marketing efforts and get a better return on investment.

iv. *Improving User Experience:*

By understanding how users interact with your site, you can make improvements to make their experience more enjoyable. For example, if you notice that users are leaving your site before completing a purchase, you can investigate why and make changes to streamline the checkout process.

In conclusion, setting up Google Analytics and Facebook Pixel on your Shopify store is a crucial step in understanding your customers, tracking your store's performance, optimizing your marketing efforts, and improving the user experience. By using these tools to understand your customers, track store performance, optimize marketing efforts, and improve the user experience, you can create a Shopify store that is not only attractive to your customers but also effective in achieving your business goals.

d. Part 4: Additional Resources

For more information on setting up Google Analytics and Facebook Pixel on Shopify, you can consult the following guides:

i. *Shopify Guide on Setting Up Google Analytics*
https://help.shopify.com/en/manual/reports-and-analytics/google-analytics/google-analytics-setup

ii. *Shopify Guide on Setting Up Facebook Pixel*
https://help.shopify.com/en/manual/promoting-marketing/analyze-marketing/meta-pixel

iii. *Google Guide on Using Google Analytics*
https://support.google.com/analytics/answer/12183125?hl=en

iv. *Facebook Guide on Setting Up Facebook Pixel*
https://www.facebook.com/business/help/952192354843755?id=1205376682832142

These guides provide detailed instructions on setting up these tools, as well as information on how to use them to improve your store.

e. Part 5: Conclusion

Setting up Google Analytics and Facebook Pixel may seem daunting at first, but once you understand how these tools work and how to use them, they can be valuable allies to help grow your Shopify store. By using these tools to understand your customers, track store performance, optimize marketing efforts, and improve the user experience, you can create a Shopify store that is not only attractive to your customers but also effective in achieving your business goals.

❖ ❖ ❖

8. Step 8: Launching Your Shopify Store

a. Part 1: Preparation for Launch

Before launching your store, it is crucial to place a few test orders to verify the proper functioning of the payment process. This allows you to ensure that your store's settings, including the payment process, order processing, inventory, shipping, and taxes, are working correctly. To place a test order, you can use Shopify Payments' test mode or use a real payment provider and immediately cancel and refund the order.

b. Part 2: Simulating Successful and Failed Transactions

It's important to simulate both successful and failed transactions to see error messages that might be displayed to a customer during payment. To simulate a successful transaction, you can add a product to your cart and go through the payment process as if you were a customer. To simulate a failed transaction, you can use specific credit card numbers to generate error messages.

c. Part 3: Removing the Password from Your Online Store

When you're ready to launch your store, you can remove

the password from your online store. During your free trial, your online store is automatically password-protected. You can remove the password from your online store from the themes page or the preferences page under the online store in your Shopify admin.

d. Part 4: Your Launch Checklist for Your Shopify Store

Before launching your store, it's helpful to have a checklist to ensure you've properly prepared your store for launch. This checklist may include items such as adding your chosen sales channels, adding a custom domain, reviewing your payment experience and options, setting up your standard pages, reviewing your email notification settings, conducting a content audit, installing an analytics tool, and optimizing for search engines (SEO).

e. Part 5: Optimizing All Images on Your Website

It's important to optimize all images on your website to ensure fast loading times. Slow-loading images can negatively impact your site's user experience and search engine performance. Shopify provides tools to help you optimize your images for the web.

f. Part 6: Conclusion

Launching your Shopify store is an exciting and significant step. By taking the time to properly prepare your store for launch, you can ensure that your store is ready to welcome customers and sell products.

9. Conclusion: Successful Launch of Your Shopify Store

Creating a Shopify store may seem like a daunting task, but with the right guidance and a bit of patience, you can create a successful online store. By following these steps, you'll be well-positioned to launch your own Shopify store and start selling products online. However, to ensure the success of your store, it's important to consider some additional elements.

a. Add Your Chosen Sales Channels

According to Statista data, the number of digital shoppers in the United States is expected to reach 291.2 million by 2025. Consumers now expect an omnichannel experience from brands. You can add available sales channels to your store. For example, eBay, Amazon, Instagram, Facebook, Google Shopping, TikTok, Buy Button, and payment links, Pinterest.

b. Add a Custom Domain

Adding a custom domain to your site gives you brand recognition and makes your URL easy to remember. You can perform a domain name search to see if your business name is available.

c. Review Your Payment Experience and Options

Before driving traffic to your store, ensure that people can actually make a purchase. According to the Baymard Institute, the documented average online shopping cart abandonment rate is nearly 70%. It's wise to address any errors and remove any friction during payment.

d. Prepare Your Standard Pages

Having a few pages that visitors can browse to learn more about your business is important. According to Shopify research, shoppers visiting a brand-new store are looking to determine if the store is a reputable business and treats its customers fairly.

e. Review Your Email Notification Settings

Make sure your customers receive order confirmations and status updates via email. You can customize these emails to match your brand.

f. Conduct a Content Audit

Review all pages on your site to ensure there are no spelling or grammar errors, all links work, and all images display correctly.

g. Install an Analytics Tool

Google Analytics is an excellent tool for tracking your store's performance. You can see how many people visit your site, how long they spend on your site, which pages they visit, and more.

h. Focus on Search Engine Optimization (SEO)

SEO is crucial for increasing your online store's visibility. Ensure your site is optimized for search engines by using relevant keywords, creating quality content, and obtaining quality backlinks.

i. Optimize All Images

Images are crucial for the user experience, especially in e-commerce. It's challenging to sell a product unless a customer can see it. However, making images smaller doesn't always improve performance. In fact, how you implement image loading can significantly impact page loading speed and layout shift. Here are some tips for optimizing images for your Shopify store:

i. Never lazy load your Largest Contentful Paint (LCP) image:
LCP is a user-centric metric that reflects page loading speed or the perception of loading speed. It's the time it takes for the largest element in the viewport to render. If you lazy load your LCP image, you have to wait for the page to render and the browser to execute the IntersectionObserver before realizing the image is visible and eventually requesting the image file. This can result in significant delay.

ii. Use native lazy loading instead of third-party libraries:
Currently, native lazy loading using the loading attribute of the <img> element is supported in browsers for 92% of global users. Thus, we recommend using native lazy loading so that 92% of users can benefit from the optimal experience.

iii. Avoid client-side rendering:
Frontend JavaScript frameworks like Vue and React have become popular in recent years, and we've seen this play out in themes. However, these frameworks can have a significant negative impact on performance. They typically send minimal HTML to the browser, which will trigger a lot of JavaScript, and then that JavaScript will render the page inside the browser. This client-side rendering pattern significantly delays the initial render.

In summary, creating a successful Shopify store requires careful planning and implementation. By following these tips, you can optimize your store to provide an exceptional user experience, improve your search engine ranking, and ultimately increase your sales. Best of luck with your Shopify journey!

CHAPTER 4: CHOOSING A NICHE FOR YOUR SHOPIFY STORE

Selecting a niche for your Shopify store is a critical step for the success of your dropshipping business. A well-chosen niche can help you target your marketing, attract the right audience, and build your brand. In essence, a niche is like a beacon that guides your business through the vast ocean of e-commerce. It allows you to focus your marketing and sales efforts on a specific market segment, which can increase the effectiveness of your campaigns and improve your return on investment.

In this chapter, we will explore how to choose a niche for your Shopify store. We'll break down the process into several steps, starting with a basic understanding of what a niche is and why it's important. Then, we'll examine how to identify a profitable niche, the factors to consider when choosing a niche, and the tools that can assist you in your research. Finally, we'll discuss the importance of validating your niche idea before fully committing to it.

This chapter is designed to be a practical guide, filled with tips and strategies that you can immediately apply to your own business. Whether you're a novice entrepreneur or an e-commerce veteran, we hope you'll find valuable insights to make an informed decision about your niche selection.

1. Understanding What a Niche Is

A niche is a specific segment of the market that you choose to target with your products. It's like a small enclave within the vast world of e-commerce where you can focus and excel. It can be a group of people, a type of product, or a specific interest. For example, if you're selling clothing, a niche could be sustainable yoga wear for women. This specificity allows you to concentrate on creating products that cater to the precise needs and desires of that group.

Understanding what a niche is can help you grasp how it can aid your business in growing and thriving. A well-defined niche can give you a clear direction for your marketing and product strategy, enabling you to target your efforts where they are most likely to bear fruit. Additionally, by focusing on a niche, you can often avoid direct competition with large e-commerce companies, which can be challenging to beat in broader markets.

You can also use this understanding to identify unique opportunities your niche may offer. Every niche has its own trends, challenges, and opportunities. By immersing yourself in your niche and learning everything you can about it, you may discover opportunities that others might miss. Whether it's a new product trend, an unmet demand, or a novel way to market your products, these opportunities can help you get ahead of the competition and grow your business.

2. Why Choosing a Niche Is Important for Your Shopify Store

Choosing a niche is crucial because it allows you to focus on a specific market segment and stand out from the competition. In the world of e-commerce, competition is fierce, and standing out can be a challenge. By selecting a specific niche, you can avoid direct competition with large companies for customer attention and instead focus on meeting the unique needs of a specific group of customers.

This can also help you target your marketing more effectively. Instead of trying to please everyone, you can create marketing messages that speak directly to your target audience. This can increase the efficiency of your marketing efforts and improve your return on investment.

Choosing a niche also allows you to concentrate on creating products that cater to the specific needs of that group. This can help you build a strong and consistent brand. For example, if you choose the niche of sustainable yoga wear for women, you can focus on creating products that are not only functional and comfortable for yoga but also durable and eco-friendly. This can help you build a strong and appealing brand for your target audience.

Furthermore, by addressing the specific needs of your niche, you can build a stronger relationship with your customers and increase their loyalty. Customers who feel that their specific needs are understood and met are more likely to return for repeat purchases and recommend your store to others. This can lead to long-term and sustainable growth for your business.

3. How to Identify a Profitable Niche

Identifying a profitable niche is a process that requires in-depth research, careful analysis, and a clear understanding of your target market. It's a crucial step that can determine the success or failure of your dropshipping business.

Understanding market trends is an essential first step. This involves examining products or product categories that are currently popular. However, it's important to distinguish sustainable trends from passing fads. A sustainable trend is more likely to provide you with a stable customer base and generate long-term sales.

Next, you need to understand the interests of your target audience. This means knowing what your potential customers are looking for, what they value, and what they are willing to buy. This can help you choose products that meet their needs and desires, increasing your chances of making sales.

Identifying product opportunities is another key factor to consider. You should look for products with high sales potential that are not already saturated in the market. This may involve researching unique products, finding ways to improve existing products, or targeting products toward a specific market segment.

To assist you in this process, you can use tools like Google Trends, Keyword Planner, and social media platforms. These tools can give you an idea of products or product categories that are currently popular and have growth potential. They can also help you identify the keywords your target audience uses to search for products, which can aid in optimizing your marketing and SEO.

Additionally, it's important to consider the profitability of the niche. This may involve examining potential profit margins, product demand, and market competition. A profitable niche will have high product demand, healthy profit margins, and moderate competition. It's also important to factor in the costs associated with running your store, such as Shopify fees, shipping costs, and marketing expenses.

Finally, it's essential to validate your niche idea before fully committing. This may involve testing your product in the market, gathering feedback from potential customers, and analyzing your competitors' performance. This validation step can help you avoid unnecessary investments in unprofitable products or markets.

In summary, identifying a profitable niche is a strategic process that requires thorough thinking, in-depth research, and careful analysis. By taking the time to do this groundwork, you can increase your chances of choosing a niche that will help you build a thriving and sustainable dropshipping business.

❖ ❖ ❖

4. Factors to Consider When Choosing a Niche

When selecting a niche for your Shopify store, it's essential to consider several key factors that can influence the success of your business. These factors may vary depending on your target market, product, and business goals, but they all play a significant role in determining the viability and profitability of your niche.

First and foremost, market size is a crucial factor. A niche with a market that's too small may not offer enough potential customers to support your business, while an overly large market may be too competitive for a new business. It's important to find a balance and choose a niche with a market size that provides growth opportunities without being oversaturated.

Secondly, product demand within your niche is also a key factor. Strong product demand indicates a healthy and active market, which can increase your chances of making sales. You can assess product demand by using tools like Google Trends, Keyword Planner, or by examining sales of similar products on Shopify or other e-commerce platforms.

Thirdly, competition within your niche is another factor to consider. Excessive competition can make it challenging to gain market share, while inadequate competition may indicate a lack of interest or demand for products in your niche. It's important to conduct competitive analysis to understand who your competitors are, what products they offer, and how you can differentiate yourself.

Fourthly, your passion for the niche topic can play a significant role in your success. Managing a Shopify store can be challenging and demanding work, and having a passion for what you do can help you stay motivated and committed. Moreover, your passion can translate into better product knowledge, a deeper understanding of customer needs, and a greater willingness to provide excellent customer service.

Finally, your ability to provide unique value to your customers is an essential factor to consider. This may involve offering unique products, providing excellent customer service, offering competitive pricing, or creating a strong brand experience. By offering unique value, you can stand out from the competition and attract and retain more customers.

In conclusion, choosing a niche for your Shopify store is a complex decision that requires thoughtful consideration and analysis. By taking these factors into account, you can increase your chances of selecting a niche that is not only profitable but also aligned with your passions and capabilities.

5. Tools to Help You Find a Niche

In the process of researching and selecting a niche for your Shopify store, several tools and resources can assist you in making an informed decision. These tools can help you identify current trends, understand product demand, analyze competition, and discover potential new niches.

Google Trends is a valuable tool that can help you understand current trends and predict future ones. It allows you to see how interest in a specific search term has evolved over time, providing insight into the popularity and demand for a particular product or niche.

Keyword Planner is another useful tool that can help you understand product demand. It enables you to search for keywords related to your niche and see how often they are searched, providing insight into the popularity and demand for those products.

Social media platforms like Facebook, Instagram, and Twitter can also be valuable tools for niche research. You can use these platforms to see which products are popular, what interests your target audience has, and how products are marketed and sold.

In addition to these tools, Shopify offers specific resources to help store owners find a niche. Shopify Compass is a learning platform that offers courses, tutorials, and webinars on various aspects of managing a Shopify store, including niche research. Exchange Marketplace is a platform where you can buy and sell Shopify stores, giving you insights into currently profitable niches.

These tools can assist you in identifying current trends, understanding product demand, analyzing competition, and discovering new potential niches that you may not have considered otherwise. By using these tools and resources, you can make a more informed decision and choose a niche with the potential for profitability and success.

6. *How to Validate Your Niche Idea*

Once you have identified a potential niche for your Shopify store, it's crucial to validate your idea before fully committing. Validating your niche idea helps confirm that your chosen niche has real potential for profitability and success. It can help you avoid costly mistakes and ensure that you're on the right track.

Testing your product in the market is an important initial step in validating your niche idea. This may involve launching a minimum viable product (MVP) version of your product or store to gauge customer reception. You can use feedback and sales data from this testing phase to assess market interest in your product and adjust your product or marketing strategy accordingly.

Collecting feedback from potential customers is another key step in validation. This can involve conducting surveys, interviews, or focus groups to understand the needs, desires, and preferences of your target audience. Customer feedback can provide valuable insights into what works and what doesn't in your niche, helping you refine your product and marketing strategy.

Analyzing the performance of your competitors is also a crucial part of niche validation. This may involve examining their products, marketing strategies, pricing, and customer feedback. This analysis can give you an idea of what works well in your niche and where there are opportunities for you to stand out.

Finally, it's essential to consider the financial aspects of your niche. This may involve conducting a cost analysis to understand the investments required to launch and operate your store and a revenue analysis to estimate the profit potential of your niche. These analyses can help you determine if your niche is financially viable and if it can support your business in the long term.

In summary, validating your niche idea is a critical step that can help you avoid costly mistakes and increase your chances of success. By taking the time to test your product, gather feedback, analyze competitors, and understand the financial aspects of your niche, you can ensure that you're making an informed and profitable choice for your Shopify store.

7. Conclusion

Choosing a niche for your Shopify store is a significant step toward the success of your business. By dedicating time to research, analyze, and validate your niche, you can increase your chances of success and stand out from the competition. Choosing a niche is an ongoing process that requires constant attention and reflection. By remaining flexible and being willing to adapt your niche as your business grows and the market evolves, you can ensure that your Shopify store remains relevant and profitable.

CHAPTER 5: HOW TO FIND DROPSHIPPING SUPPLIERS

Dropshipping is a popular business model that has revolutionized the way e-commerce is conducted. It offers a unique opportunity for entrepreneurs to launch an online business without the need to invest in initial inventory, thus eliminating one of the major barriers to entry into the retail world.

In the dropshipping model, as a retailer, you don't keep the products you sell in stock. Instead, when you sell a product, you purchase the item from a third party—usually a wholesaler or manufacturer—who then ships the product directly to your customer. This means you can focus on the marketing and sales aspects of your business without worrying about the logistics of storage or shipping.

However, while dropshipping may seem simple on the surface, the success of a dropshipping business largely depends on the choice of suppliers. A good supplier will not only be able to provide you with high-quality products at competitive prices, but they will also be reliable in terms of meeting delivery deadlines and efficiently handling returns and claims.

Selecting a dropshipping supplier is not a decision to be taken lightly. It's a choice that can have a significant impact on the viability and profitability of your business. This chapter aims to guide you through the process of researching and selecting dropshipping suppliers, providing practical advice and strategies to help you make the best choice for your business.

1. Understanding the Role of Suppliers in Dropshipping

In the dropshipping model, suppliers are not just sellers; they are key partners in your business. Their role goes far beyond simply providing products. They are responsible for manufacturing and shipping products directly to customers on your behalf, making them an essential link in your supply chain.

Dropshipping suppliers work behind the scenes of your business. While you focus on building your brand and acquiring customers, they handle production, packaging, shipping, and sometimes even after-sales service. This means that the quality of the products your customers receive, the speed at which they receive them, and how issues are resolved are all largely determined by your suppliers.

That's why it's crucial to choose suppliers who can not only deliver high-quality products but are also reliable and efficient. A good dropshipping supplier will be able to meet delivery deadlines, handle returns and exchanges efficiently, and offer excellent customer service. They should also be able to adapt to your evolving needs as your business grows.

In the end, your suppliers are an extension of your business. Their performance directly impacts customer satisfaction and, consequently, the success of your business. Understanding their crucial role and carefully selecting your partners can make all the difference between success and failure in the world of dropshipping.

2. Different Platforms for Finding Suppliers

In the world of dropshipping, there are numerous online platforms that facilitate the search and selection of suppliers. These platforms vary in terms of size, scope, types of products offered, and additional services they may provide. Here's a more detailed overview of some of these platforms:

a. Alibaba:

Alibaba is one of the world's largest B2B platforms, connecting buyers to manufacturers and suppliers worldwide. With a vast range of products and suppliers, Alibaba offers great flexibility for dropshipping businesses. However, it's important to note that most suppliers on Alibaba are based in Asia, which can lead to longer delivery times.

b. AliExpress:

A subsidiary of Alibaba, AliExpress operates more like a B2C platform, allowing dropshipping businesses to purchase products individually. It's a popular option for those starting in dropshipping due to its user-friendly interface and low minimum order requirements.

c. SaleHoo:

SaleHoo is a directory of wholesalers and dropshipping suppliers that provides access to over 8,000 international suppliers. SaleHoo stands out for its strong customer service and educational resources to help new entrepreneurs succeed.

d. Doba:

Doba is a dropshipping platform that offers access to millions of products from hundreds of suppliers. With Doba, you can search for products, manage your suppliers and inventory, and place orders directly from the platform.

In addition to these platforms, there are other options that may be more suitable for specific needs:

e. Automizely:

Automizely is a dropshipping platform that focuses on simplifying the process of finding products to sell online. With Automizely, you can access a wide variety of products on AliExpress with just a few clicks, making it easy to add new products to your store.

f. Printful:

Printful is an on-demand dropshipping service specializing in custom products. With Printful, your customers can choose from a range of artwork to be printed on products like sweatshirts, T-shirts, laptop cases, and more. It's an excellent option for businesses looking to offer personalized products.

g. DropnShop:

DropnShop is a dropshipping app designed specifically for online stores selling French products. It offers products from leading French manufacturers and provides thousands of references in various categories. It's a great option for those targeting the French market.

h. Glowroad:

Glowroad is a Shopify dropshipping app that focuses on the Indian market. With Glowroad, you can ship items to the UK, US, Australia, Canada, and over 30 countries. It's an interesting option for those looking to target the Indian market.

In addition to these platforms, there are also other options worth exploring:

i. Spocket:

Spocket is a dropshipping platform that focuses on suppliers based in the United States and Europe. This can help reduce delivery times and offer higher-quality products. Spocket also offers easy integration with e-commerce platforms like Shopify and WooCommerce.

j. Oberlo:

Oberlo is another popular platform that integrates directly with Shopify. It allows entrepreneurs to find products to sell online from various suppliers worldwide. Oberlo also provides tools to assist with product pricing, inventory management, and shipping.

k. Modalyst:

Modalyst is a dropshipping platform that offers a range of high-quality products from independent suppliers and designer brands. Modalyst stands out for its selection of unique products that can help your online store stand out.

1. **Dropified:**

Dropified is a dropshipping platform that offers tools to automate many aspects of your dropshipping business. With Dropified, you can automate adding new products, order management, shipment tracking, and more.

It's important to note that each platform has its own advantages and disadvantages, and what works best for you will depend on your specific needs as a dropshipping business. Therefore, it's crucial to conduct thorough research and test different platforms before making a decision.

3. How to Contact Suppliers

Once you have identified potential suppliers for your dropshipping business, the next step is to get in touch with them. This step is crucial because it allows you to ask relevant questions to assess whether a supplier is the right choice for your business. For example, you can inquire about their average delivery times, return and refund policies, production capabilities, and quality standards.

When contacting a supplier, it's important to present yourself professionally. Clearly explain who you are, what your business does, and what your product needs are. Make sure to ask specific questions to gather all the necessary information. For example, you can ask:

- What are your average delivery times?
- What is your return and refund policy?
- What is your production capacity?
- How do you ensure the quality of your products?
- What are your prices, and do you offer discounts for bulk orders?

It's also recommended to request product samples to evaluate quality. This can help you determine if the products meet your standards and your customers' expectations.

Finally, don't forget to discuss payment terms and understand how and when the supplier expects to be paid. This can vary from one supplier to another, so it's important to clarify this from the beginning to avoid misunderstandings or potential issues in the future.

4. How to Negotiate with Suppliers

Negotiating with suppliers is an essential skill for any dropshipping entrepreneur. It can help you secure better terms, lower prices, shorter delivery times, and higher product quality. Here are some tips for negotiating effectively with your suppliers:

a. **Prepare Yourself:**

Before starting negotiations, do your research. Understand the market, average prices, delivery times, and quality standards for the products you want to sell. This will give you a stronger negotiating position.

b. Be Clear About Your Expectations:

When negotiating with a supplier, be clear about what you expect from them. Whether it's about price, quality, delivery times, or after-sales service, make sure the supplier understands your expectations.

c. Negotiate on Multiple Fronts:

Don't focus solely on price. While product cost is important, other factors can also be negotiated, such as delivery times, payment terms, product quality, and more.

d. Build a Relationship:

Negotiation is not just about numbers; it's also about building relationships. Try to establish a positive relationship with your suppliers. This can lead to better long-term conditions.

e. Be Prepared to Compromise:

Negotiation is a give-and-take process. You may not be able to get everything you want, so be prepared to make compromises. However, make sure the compromises you make don't compromise the quality of your products or the service you provide to your customers.

f. Formalize the Agreement:

Once you've reached an agreement, make sure to formalize it in writing. This can take the form of a contract or a purchase agreement. Ensure that all details of the agreement are clearly stated, and both parties understand their obligations.

Finally, remember that negotiation is an ongoing process. Market conditions, production costs, and other factors can change, so it's important to regularly review your agreements with suppliers.

◆ ◆ ◆

5. Common Mistakes to Avoid When Selecting Suppliers

Selecting suppliers is a crucial step in the process of creating a dropshipping business. However, there are several common mistakes that entrepreneurs often make during this step. Here are some of these mistakes and how to avoid them:

a. Choosing Suppliers Based Solely on Price:

While price is an important factor, it should not be the sole criterion for selection. A supplier offering low prices may not be able to provide consistent quality or reliable delivery. Therefore, it's essential to consider other factors such as product quality, delivery reliability, and customer service.

b. Not Checking Product Quality:

The quality of the products you sell will directly impact customer satisfaction and your business's reputation. Therefore, it's crucial to check the quality of a supplier's products before deciding to work with them. This may involve requesting product samples, checking quality certifications, or reading reviews from other customers.

c. Not Building Good Relationships with Suppliers:

A good relationship with your suppliers can help you obtain better terms, quickly resolve issues, and receive more personalized service. So, it's important to communicate regularly with your suppliers, treat them with respect, and aim to build a trusting relationship.

d. Ignoring Supplier Ratings and Reviews:

Supplier ratings and reviews can give you insights into their reliability, product quality, and customer service. It's important to take the time to read these ratings and reviews before choosing a supplier.

e. Not Having a Backup Plan:

Even with the best supplier, unexpected issues such as delivery delays or quality problems can arise. Therefore, it's important to have a backup plan, such as a second supplier, in place to avoid these issues affecting your business.

By avoiding these mistakes, you can increase your chances of selecting the right suppliers for your dropshipping business, ensuring customer satisfaction and the success of your business.

6. Additional Tips for Finding Dropshipping Suppliers

ccording to a YouTube video by Austin Raven, here are some additional tips for finding dropshipping suppliers:

a. Work with a Freight Forwarder:

A freight forwarder is a company that handles the shipping of products from the factory to your customer. They can communicate directly with manufacturers, negotiate prices, and handle custom packaging. They typically have better communication and care more about you than manufacturers.

b. Don't Rely Solely on One Website to Find a Supplier:

Whether it's AliExpress, Spocket, ZenDrop, or any other site, they all have good suppliers, but you need to take the time to find them. It's a numbers game, so don't hesitate to contact many suppliers.

c. Check Shipping Routes:

Some suppliers may have faster shipping routes available, but they may not list them on their product page. You'll need to contact them directly to get this information.

d. Request Product Samples:

Before deciding to work with a supplier, request product samples. This allows you to check the quality of the products and ensure they meet your expectations.

e. Build Good Relationships with Your Suppliers:

A strong relationship with your suppliers can help you secure better prices and quickly resolve any issues that may arise. It's important to communicate regularly with your suppliers and treat them as partners rather than mere suppliers.

f. Ask for Volume Order Discounts:

If you plan to provide a consistent volume of orders to your suppliers, ask if they can offer you discounts. This can help increase your profit margins.

g. Check if the Supplier Offers Product Customization:

If you want to build a brand, it may be helpful to work with a supplier that offers product customization, such as printing your logo on the products.

h. Order Products to Your Address Without Informing the Supplier:

This allows you to check the quality of packaging and delivery times without the supplier knowing it's a test order.

7. Conclusion

Researching and selecting reliable and high-quality dropshipping suppliers are essential steps to ensure the success of any e-commerce business. It's a process that requires time, patience, and careful attention to detail. It's not just about finding suppliers who can offer competitive prices;

it's also about finding partners who understand your business goals, are committed to quality and service excellence, and can work with you to help your business grow and thrive.

By asking the right questions, carefully evaluating the answers, and establishing strong and mutually beneficial relationships with your suppliers, you can create a solid foundation for your dropshipping business. This can not only help you avoid common problems that can hinder your business's growth but also allow you to quickly adapt to market changes, expand your product range, and improve your customer service.

Ultimately, the success of your dropshipping business depends on the quality of the partnerships you establish with your suppliers. By choosing the right partners, you can create a dropshipping business that not only meets your customers' needs but is also sustainable and capable of thriving in an ever-changing business environment.

CHAPTER 6: HOW TO ADD PRODUCTS TO YOUR SHOPIFY STORE

Adding products to your Shopify store is a crucial step in setting up your e-commerce business. It's through your products that you can showcase what you have to offer to your customers and encourage them to make purchases. This guide will walk you through the process of adding products to your Shopify store, step by step.

1. Adding Products via Shopify

a. **Step 1: Access the Product Page**

The first step to adding products to your Shopify store is to access the product page. Log in to your Shopify account and go to your dashboard. On the left side of your dashboard, you will see a navigation menu. Click on "Products" in this menu to access the product page. Here, you will see a list of all the products you've already added to your store.

b. **Step 2: Add a New Product**

Once you're on the product page, you can start adding a new

product to your store. To do this, click on the "Add a product" button located at the top right of the page. This will redirect you to a new page where you can enter your product details.

c. Step 3: Enter Product Details

On the product addition page, you'll need to enter several details about your product. These details include:

i. *Product Title: This is the name of your product. It should be descriptive and appealing to your customers.*
ii. *Description: This is where you can provide more details about your product. You can include information about the product's features, usage, benefits, etc.*
iii. *Images: You can upload images of your product here. Ensure that your images are of high quality and showcase your product from different angles.*
iv. *Price: This is the price at which you're selling your product. You can also add a compare-at price if your product is on sale.*
v. *Inventory: Here, you can manage your stock. You can add a Stock Keeping Unit (SKU), a barcode, and the quantity of available products.*
vi. *Shipping: This section allows you to manage your product's shipping information. You can add the product's weight, packaging size, and determine if the product requires physical shipping.*
vii. *Product Variants: If your product comes in different variants (e.g., different sizes or colors), you can add them here.*

d. Step 4: Configure Product Visibility

Once you've entered all the necessary product details, you can configure its visibility. You can choose whether you want your product to be visible on your online store, and you can also decide if you want it available on various sales channels, such as Facebook or Amazon.

e. Step 5: Save the Product

After entering all the required information and configuring your product's visibility, don't forget to click "Save" to add the product to your store. The "Save" button is located at the top right of the product addition page.

f. Step 6: Repeat the Process

Now that you've added a product to your Shopify store, you can repeat this process for any other products you want to add. Each product will require the same basic information, but remember that each product is unique and may require additional details based on its nature.

2. Adding Products via the Shopify Mobile App

In addition to the web interface, Shopify also offers a mobile app that allows you to add products to your store directly from your smartphone. The app is available for both iOS and Android and provides a user-friendly interface for adding products. You can add products to your store by following the same steps as on the web interface, but from your phone.

3. Bulk Product Addition

If you have a large number of products to add to your store, it may be more efficient to add products in bulk. Shopify allows for bulk product import using a CSV file. You can create a CSV file with all the information about your products and import it into Shopify, adding all your products at once. This can be a considerable time saver if you have hundreds or thousands of products to add.

❖ ❖ ❖

4. Managing Digital Products

If you're selling digital products like e-books or online courses, the product addition process is slightly different. Shopify offers a free app called "Digital Downloads" that allows you to add digital products to your store. Once the app is installed, you can add digital products in the same way you add physical products, but you'll also have the option to upload digital files that customers can download after purchase.

❖ ❖ ❖

5. Using the Shopify API

For more advanced users, Shopify offers an API that allows you to programmatically add products to your store. This can be useful if you have a large quantity of products to add or if you want to automate the product addition process. Using the Shopify API requires programming skills, so if you're not comfortable with that, consider hiring a developer to assist you.

◆ ◆ ◆

6. Adding Products via Dedicated Dropshipping Platform Plugins

a. DSers

DSers is a qualified order management tool and one of the most well-known and reliable dropshipping partners from AliExpress. It offers a variety of features, including supplier optimization, bulk order management, inventory management, managing multiple stores, automatic order status updates, automatic pricing, variant mapping, and more.

b. DSM Tool

DSM Tool is another dropshipping platform that integrates with eBay and Shopify. It automates order fulfillment within a short period, from 7 to 15 days. Its key features include bulk product importing, sourcing high-quality products, advanced product editing, listing SEO optimization, automatic restocking, and an affiliate program.

c. Trendsi

Trendsi is a dropshipping app that allows you to sell trendy fashion clothing, shoes, and accessories directly from your Shopify store. The app offers wholesale pricing on all its products, enabling you to achieve higher profit margins.

d. CJ Dropshipping

As mentioned earlier, CJ Dropshipping is a dropshipping platform that integrates with Shopify. CJ Dropshipping allows you to find products from various suppliers and add them to your Shopify store.

e. DropCommerce

DropCommerce is another Shopify dropshipping app that stands out because it only offers products from North American suppliers. This means shorter delivery times and often higher product quality.

f. GlowRoad

GlowRoad is a dropshipping app that enables you to find and sell products across various categories. With GlowRoad, you can add products to your Shopify store with just one click.

g. Spocket

Spocket is a dropshipping platform that lets you choose the best products to sell from various suppliers worldwide. You can try Spocket for free, and if you decide to subscribe to a paid plan, you can access additional features.

h. Zendrop

Zendrop is an automated dropshipping solution that allows

you to find and add products to your Shopify store in a few clicks. Zendrop also offers fast order fulfillment and top-notch customer service.

i. Importify

Importify enables you to import products from various e-commerce platforms directly into your Shopify store. With Importify, you can also automate the order placement process.

j. Modalyst

Modalyst is a dropshipping platform that focuses on branded products, fashion items, luxury goods, and unique niche products. With Modalyst, you can add products to your Shopify store with a single click.

k. Inventory Source

Inventory Source is a dropshipping platform that allows you to automatically sync products and inventory from your suppliers with your Shopify store.

l. Syncee

Syncee is a dropshipping app that lets you find and add products to your Shopify store from suppliers worldwide. Syncee also integrates with several other e-commerce platforms.

m. Oberlo

Oberlo is one of the most popular dropshipping apps for Shopify. It makes it easy to import products directly from suppliers into your Shopify store and fulfill orders directly to your customers.

n. Printful

Printful is a dropshipping app that specializes in print-on-demand products. With Printful, you can sell custom-printed items like t-shirts, hoodies, posters, mugs, bags, and more.

o. Aliexpress Dropshipping

Aliexpress Dropshipping is an app that allows you to add products from Aliexpress to your Shopify store. It offers full integration with Aliexpress, meaning you can import products, manage orders, and track shipments directly from your Shopify dashboard.

Each plugin has its own features and benefits, so it's important to choose the one that best fits your specific needs. Remember that adding products to your store is an important step, but it's also essential to maintain a good relationship with your suppliers, efficiently manage your inventory, and provide excellent customer service.

7. Conclusion

Adding products to your Shopify store is an ongoing task. As you add new products to your store, you'll need to continue managing and updating your product listings to ensure they are up-to-date and accurate. By following the steps outlined in this guide, you should be able to add products to your store efficiently and effectively.

CHAPTER 7: HOW TO SET UP PAYMENT AND SHIPPING SETTINGS ON SHOPIFY

1. Setting Up Payment Settings on Shopify

Configuring payment settings on Shopify is a crucial step to ensure the smooth operation of your online store. Here's a detailed guide to help you through this process:

a. Access Your Payment Settings:

To begin, log in to your Shopify account. Once you're on your dashboard, look for the "Settings" section located at the bottom left of the screen. Click on it, then select "Payments." You will be redirected to the payment settings page.

b. Choose Your Payment Provider:

Shopify offers a variety of payment providers to cater to different merchants' needs. You can choose to use Shopify Payments, which is Shopify's default payment provider. However, if you prefer, you can also choose from a list of third-party payment providers. Each provider has its own advantages and disadvantages, so be sure to do your research to find the one that best suits your business.

c. Configure Your Payment Settings:

Once you've chosen your payment provider, you need to configure your payment settings. This may include adding your bank account information, configuring your credit card settings, and setting up alternative payment settings. Take the time to fill in this information carefully to avoid payment issues in the future.

d. Save Your Settings:

After configuring your payment settings, don't forget to click "Save" to save your changes. This will ensure that all your payment settings are correctly saved and ready to use.

2. Setting Up Shipping Settings on Shopify

Configuring shipping settings on Shopify is just as important as configuring payment settings. Here's how you can do it:

a. Access Your Shipping Settings:

Log in to your Shopify account and go to the "Settings" section. Then, click on "Shipping and delivery." You will be redirected to the shipping settings page.

b. Configure Your Shipping Zones:

Shipping zones are geographical regions where you ship

your products. You can set up different shipping zones based on your needs. For each shipping zone, you can define specific shipping rates. This allows you to control shipping costs for different regions and offer competitive shipping rates to your customers.

c. Configure Your Shipping Rates:

For each shipping zone, you can configure different shipping rates. You can set fixed shipping rates, rates based on weight or price, or rates calculated based on your carrier's rates. This gives you great flexibility in determining how you want to charge for shipping to your customers.

d. Configure Your Delivery Settings:

In addition to standard shipping settings, Shopify also allows you to set up local delivery options for customers located near your location. This can include local delivery and in-store pickup. These options can provide added convenience to your customers and may help boost sales.

e. Save Your Settings:

Once you've configured your shipping settings, don't forget to click "Save" to save your changes. This will ensure that all your shipping settings are correctly saved and ready to use.

By following these steps, you can effectively configure your payment and shipping settings on Shopify. However, keep in mind that these settings may require adjustments over time based on changing business needs and customer preferences. Therefore, it's important to review them regularly to ensure they are always optimized for your online store.

CHAPTER 8: HOW TO CHOOSE AND CUSTOMIZE A THEME FOR YOUR SHOPIFY STORE

The choice of your Shopify store's theme is a crucial step in creating your online store. It's about more than just selecting attractive colors and designs. A good theme is the foundation of your store's visual identity, and it plays a pivotal role in how your customers perceive and interact with your brand.

When chosen wisely, a theme can help attract and retain customers by creating a strong and positive first impression. It can showcase your products, make navigation easier, and make the buying process as simple and enjoyable as possible. Furthermore, a well-designed and structured theme can contribute to increased sales by encouraging visitors to explore your store and discover your products.

Lastly, a good theme can enhance the user experience by providing an intuitive and responsive interface. It can help your customers easily find what they're looking for, clearly understand what you offer, and complete their purchases smoothly. In summary, the theme's choice is a strategic decision that can have a significant impact on the success of your Shopify store.

❖ ❖ ❖

1. Why Theme Selection is Crucial for Your Shopify Store

A well-chosen theme is more than just a skin for your Shopify store; it's the central element that can make the difference between a store that converts and one that doesn't. It plays a crucial role in several aspects of your online store.

Firstly, your theme is often the first thing your customers see when they visit your store. It contributes to creating a positive and memorable first impression. An attractive, professional design that aligns with your brand can immediately grab visitors' attention and encourage them to explore your store further.

Secondly, your theme is a powerful tool for strengthening your brand. It allows you to create a consistent and recognizable visual identity that reflects your brand's values and essence. Colors, fonts, images, and even the layout of elements can all be used to tell your brand's story and establish an emotional connection with your customers.

Lastly, a good theme streamlines navigation for your customers. It organizes information logically and intuitively, making it easy for customers to find what they're looking for. A well-structured theme can guide visitors through your store, lead them to products or information they seek, and prompt them to take the desired action, whether it's purchasing a product, signing up for a newsletter, or contacting you. In essence, theme selection is a strategic decision that directly impacts your customers' experience, your brand's image, and ultimately, the success of your Shopify store.

2. How to Choose the Right Theme for Your Shopify Store

a. Understand Your Target Audience

The first step in choosing the right theme for your Shopify store is to understand who your customers are and what they expect from an online store. It's crucial to consider their preferences, buying behaviors, and user experience expectations. For example, if you sell luxury products, you might want a theme that reflects this upscale image with an elegant design and premium features. If your target audience is young and trendy, a modern, colorful, and dynamic theme might be more suitable. It's also important to stay updated on current web and e-commerce design trends as they can influence your target audience's expectations.

b. Identify Your Feature Needs

Every online store has specific feature requirements based on its industry, products, and sales strategy. Some Shopify themes offer specific features like product galleries, blog sections, or social media integrations. Identify the features you need before choosing a theme. For instance, if you have a wide range of products, you might require a theme with extensive filtering and sorting options. If you plan to regularly publish content, a theme with a robust blog section could be preferable.

c. Consider Design and Aesthetics

Your store's design should be visually appealing and align with your brand. Take into account the colors, fonts, and the overall style of the theme. A theme that matches your brand identity can help create a consistent experience for your customers, reinforce brand recognition, and establish an emotional connection with them. Remember that your store's design should also facilitate navigation and highlight your products.

d. Mobile Compatibility

With the rise of mobile commerce, it's essential that your online store is optimized for mobile devices. Ensure that the theme you choose is responsive, meaning it automatically adapts to the user's screen size and provides a good mobile experience. A theme that's not optimized for mobile devices can frustrate users and deter them from making purchases.

e. Review Ratings and Reviews

User reviews can give you insights into the quality of a theme and its customer service. Look for a theme with good ratings and positive reviews. Don't forget to check how the theme developer responds to user comments and concerns, as this can give you an idea of their customer service quality. Additionally, it can be helpful to see how the theme performs in action. Search for examples of online stores using the theme you're interested in. This can give you a better idea of what to expect and how you can customize the theme to meet your own needs.

In summary, theme selection is a strategic decision with a direct impact on your customers' experience, your brand's image, and ultimately, the success of your Shopify store. Take the time to research, evaluate your options, and choose a theme that aligns with your vision and business goals.

It's important to note that theme selection isn't a final decision.

Shopify allows you to change your theme at any time, so you can experiment with different themes and see which one works best for your store. However, a theme change may require adjustments and customizations, so it's best to make the right choice from the start.

In the end, the perfect theme for your Shopify store is the one that meets your needs, appeals to your target audience, and helps grow your business.

3. How to Customize Your Shopify Theme

a. Modify General Settings

Most Shopify themes allow you to modify general settings such as colors, fonts, and logos. These changes may seem minor, but they can have a significant impact on your store's appearance and usability. For example, you can choose colors that match your brand identity, select easily readable fonts, and upload your logo to enhance brand recognition. Furthermore, many themes allow you to customize buttons, borders, backgrounds, and other design elements to create a consistent user experience.

b. Customize Store Sections

Each Shopify theme has sections like the header, footer, homepage, product pages, and more. You can customize these sections to fit your needs. For instance, you can add banners or sliders to your homepage to showcase your best-selling products or promotions. You can also change the layout of your product pages to highlight your product images and make the purchasing process smoother. Remember that each section of your store should serve a specific purpose and contribute to the overall customer experience.

c. Add Functionality with Apps

If you require additional functionality that isn't included in your theme, you can add Shopify apps. There are thousands of available apps that can enhance your store's capabilities, such as email marketing tools, social media integrations, SEO tools, shipping options, and more. When choosing apps, make sure they are compatible with your theme and can improve your customers' experience.

d. Test and Optimize Your Theme

Once you've customized your theme, it's essential to test it to ensure it functions correctly and provides a good user experience. Check your store on different devices and browsers to ensure it's responsive and works properly. Use analytics tools to monitor how your customers interact with your store and identify areas that can be improved.

Customizing your Shopify theme is an ongoing process. As your business grows and your customers' needs evolve, you may need to make changes and adjustments to your theme to ensure it remains effective and attractive.

❖ ❖ ❖

4. Best Practices for Theme Customization

When customizing your theme, it's essential to keep the user experience in mind. Here are some best practices to follow:

a. Prioritize Ease of Navigation

Ensure that your store is easy to navigate. Customers should be able to quickly and easily find what they're looking for. This means organizing your products logically, using clear menus and effective search filters, and providing links to important information like return policies and contact details. Intuitive navigation can help increase time spent on your site, reduce bounce rates, and boost conversions.

b. Highlight Important Information

Critical information should be easy to find. This includes product details, prices, shipping, and payment options, as well as customer reviews. Make sure this information is presented clearly and concisely and is easily accessible from every product page. Additionally, include clear calls to action to guide customers to the next step, whether it's adding a product to the cart, continuing shopping, or proceeding to checkout.

c. Maintain Design Consistency

Keep your design consistent to strengthen your brand. This means using the same colors, fonts, and graphic styles across all your pages. Design consistency can help create a smooth user experience, reinforce brand recognition, and establish an emotional connection with your customers. Furthermore, consistent design can make your store look more professional and trustworthy.

d. Optimize for Mobile

With the increase in mobile commerce, it's crucial to optimize your store for mobile devices. Ensure that your theme is responsive, automatically adapting to different screen sizes. Additionally, make sure interactive elements like buttons and links are large and spaced out enough for easy use on touchscreens.

e. Test and Adjust Regularly

Finally, remember that customizing your theme is an ongoing process. Regularly test your store to ensure it functions correctly and provides a good user experience. Use analytics tools to track user behavior, identify issues and opportunities, and make adjustments accordingly.

5. Conclusion

Choosing and customizing a theme is an important and exciting step in creating your Shopify store. With the right theme, you can build an attractive store that reflects your brand, meets your customers' needs, and helps increase your sales. It's a unique opportunity to bring your vision to life and create an online shopping experience that is not only functional but also memorable and engaging.

A well-chosen and customized theme can make the difference between a store that converts and one that doesn't. It can help create a positive first impression, strengthen your brand, and facilitate navigation for your customers. It can also enhance the user experience by making your store easy to navigate and showcasing your products attractively.

However, theme selection and customization are not tasks to be taken lightly. They require strategic thinking, a clear understanding of your target audience and business goals, and a willingness to experiment and optimize based on customer feedback and store performance.

In the end, the perfect theme for your Shopify store is the one that helps you tell your brand's story, engage your customers, and encourage them to return time and time again. So, take the time to choose wisely, customize carefully, and test regularly. Your Shopify store is a reflection of your online business, and a well-chosen and customized theme can help you shine.

CHAPTER 9: HOW TO OPTIMIZE YOUR SHOPIFY STORE FOR SEO

1. Introduction to SEO Optimization for Shopify

Search Engine Optimization (SEO) is an essential component for any online store, including those hosted on Shopify. SEO involves a series of techniques and strategies used to enhance a website's visibility in search engine results like Google, Bing, or Yahoo. The goal is to attract high-quality traffic, meaning visitors actively interested in the products or services you offer.

In an increasingly competitive digital landscape, a solid SEO strategy can make the difference between a thriving online store and one struggling to attract and retain customers. A well-optimized store for SEO can lead to a significant increase in organic traffic—visitors who arrive at your site after conducting a search on a search engine—and potentially boost sales.

Shopify, as a leading e-commerce platform, recognizes the importance of SEO for its users' success. That's why the platform offers a variety of built-in tools and features to help you optimize your store for SEO. These tools range from editing title and description tags to customizing URLs and even automatically generating sitemap files. Additionally, Shopify also provides a range of third-party apps that can further enhance your SEO efforts.

It's important to note that SEO is not a one-time process but rather a long-term strategy that requires ongoing monitoring and adjustments. Search engine algorithms continually evolve, so staying up-to-date with SEO best practices is crucial for maintaining your online store's visibility.

2. The Importance of SEO for Your Shopify Store

SEO is critically important for your Shopify store for several reasons. First and foremost, an effective SEO strategy can significantly increase the amount of traffic you receive from search engines. The higher you rank in search results, the more likely you are to attract visitors to your store. This can lead to a significant increase in potential customers discovering your products.

But SEO doesn't just increase the quantity of traffic—it also enhances the quality of that traffic. Users who find your store through organic search are often more engaged and more likely to make a purchase since they were actively searching for a product you sell. In other words, SEO helps you attract visitors who are already interested in what you have to offer, increasing your conversion chances.

Moreover, SEO is a long-term strategy that can yield lasting benefits for your store. Unlike paid advertising, which only generates traffic as long as you continue to pay, the efforts you put into SEO can continue to pay off for months or even years.

Once you've achieved a good ranking in search results, you can keep attracting organic traffic without additional spending.

Lastly, it's essential to recognize that SEO can also contribute to your brand's credibility and trustworthiness. Users tend to trust sites that appear at the top of search results, so ranking well for relevant keywords can help enhance your store's reputation.

In summary, SEO is a fundamental element of a successful e-commerce strategy. It can help you attract more visitors, improve the quality of your traffic, build trust in your brand, and ensure long-term growth for your Shopify store.

3. How to Add Keywords for SEO on Shopify

Adding keywords is a fundamental step in SEO optimization. Keywords are the terms users enter into search engines when looking for a product or service. They are essential for helping search engines understand your site's content and when it should appear in search results.

To add keywords to your Shopify store, you need to incorporate them into various elements of your site. Here's how you can do it:

a. Product Titles

Product titles are one of the primary places where you should include keywords. They carry significant weight with search engines and are often the first thing users see in search results.

b. Product Descriptions

Product descriptions offer another important opportunity to include keywords. Try to naturally integrate keywords into detailed and informative descriptions that provide real value to users.

c. Meta Tags

Meta tags, including title and description tags, are another key element for keyword optimization. They appear in your site's code and in search results, influencing your visibility.

d. URL

Keywords can also be optimized in your product page URLs. A descriptive URL rich in keywords can help both search engines and users understand the page's content.

e. Alt Text for Images

Search engines cannot "see" images, so they rely on alt text to understand what they represent. Make sure to include relevant keywords in your alt text.

When choosing and using keywords, ensure they are relevant to the products you sell. Use keyword research tools to find terms with high search volume but low to moderate competition. Additionally, try to utilize long-tail keywords—phrases of three words or more that are highly specific to what you sell. These types of keywords are typically less competitive and can help you target specific niches.

In summary, adding keywords is a crucial step in SEO optimization on Shopify. By strategically incorporating relevant keywords into your store, you can improve your visibility in search engines and attract more potential customers.

4. Site Optimization for SEO

Optimizing your site for SEO is a multifaceted process that goes beyond keyword addition. It involves creating a site that is not only search-engine-friendly but also useful and appealing to real visitors to your site. Here are some key aspects of site optimization for SEO:

a. Easy Navigation

A well-structured and easy-to-navigate site is essential for a good user experience, which can positively impact your SEO ranking. This includes having a clear site hierarchy, intuitive menus, and internal links that help users find what they're looking for. Additionally, good navigation aids search engines in understanding and indexing your site more efficiently.

b. Site Speed

The loading speed of your site is a significant ranking factor for Google. Sites that load quickly provide a better user experience and, as a result, are favored by search engines. You can optimize your site's speed by reducing image sizes, minimizing CSS and JavaScript code, and using a fast and well-coded Shopify theme.

c. Mobile Compatibility

With the increasing use of smartphones, a significant portion of online searches is done on mobile devices. Google has adopted a mobile-first indexing approach, meaning it considers your site's mobile version for ranking. Ensure your site is responsive, meaning it adapts well to all screen types, and provides a quality user experience on mobile.

d. Image Optimization

Images can play a crucial role in SEO. Ensure they are of high quality and optimized for the web, including reduced file size and the appropriate format. Don't forget to add descriptive alt tags containing keywords to help search engines understand image content.

e. Quality Content

The content on your site should be high-quality, relevant, and valuable to your visitors. This includes product descriptions, blog posts, guides, and more. Good content can help position you as an authority in your field, attract and retain visitors, and improve your SEO ranking.

In summary, site optimization for SEO is a complex process that requires attention to many details. However, by taking the time to do things right, you can improve the visibility of your Shopify store, provide a better user experience, and ultimately increase your sales.

5. SEO Checklist for Shopify Online Stores

Optimizing your Shopify store for SEO may seem like a daunting task, but by breaking down the process into manageable steps, you can make your site more visible to search engines. Here's a detailed checklist to help you get started:

a. Use Relevant Keywords

Incorporate relevant keywords into product titles, descriptions, URLs, and image alt text. These keywords should reflect what potential customers might use to search for the products you sell.

b. Ensure Your Site Is Easily Navigable

A clear site structure and intuitive navigation are crucial to helping users and search engines find what they're looking for. This includes using clear menus, internal links, and a logical site hierarchy.

c. Optimize Your Site's Speed

Search engines favor fast-loading sites. You can optimize your site's speed by compressing images, minimizing CSS and JavaScript code, and choosing a Shopify theme designed for speed.

d. Make Your Site Mobile-Friendly

As more people shop on mobile devices, ensure your site is

responsive and provides a quality user experience on all screen types. Google considers the mobile version of your site for ranking.

e. Use Unique Meta Tags for Each Page

Meta tags, including titles and descriptions, are displayed in search results and can influence click-through rates. Each page on your site should have unique meta tags that accurately describe the page's content.

f. Add a Sitemap to Your Shopify Store

A sitemap helps Google understand your site's structure and index your pages correctly. Shopify automatically generates a sitemap for your store, but you should submit it to Google Search Console for recognition.

g. Use Google Analytics to Track Your SEO Performance

Google Analytics is a powerful tool that can help you understand how users interact with your site and identify opportunities for improvement. Use it to track keyword rankings, organic search traffic, user behavior, and more.

By following this checklist, you can ensure that you cover the essentials of SEO optimization for your Shopify store. Remember that SEO is an ongoing process—it's essential to regularly monitor your performance and make adjustments as needed.

6. Conclusion

Search Engine Optimization (SEO) is not a task you can simply check off your list once it's done. It's an ongoing process that requires constant attention, monitoring, and regular adjustments to remain effective. Search engine algorithms constantly evolve, and user search behaviors change over time. This means you must stay vigilant and be ready to adapt your SEO strategy accordingly.

However, despite the work and commitment it requires, SEO is an investment worth making. By taking the time to optimize your Shopify store for SEO, you can improve your visibility on search engines, leading to a significant increase in traffic to your site. And it's not just any traffic—it's qualified traffic, composed of people actively interested in what you have to offer.

More visibility and qualified traffic can translate into increased sales and revenue for your Shopify store. Beyond that, a robust SEO strategy can also contribute to the credibility and trust in your brand, enhance the user experience on your site, and position you as an authority in your industry.

In the end, SEO is an essential component of any successful e-commerce strategy. By investing in SEO, you're investing in long-term visibility and success for your Shopify store.

CHAPTER 10: HOW TO SET UP GOOGLE ANALYTICS AND META PIXEL FOR YOUR SHOPIFY STORE

In the world of e-commerce, knowledge is power. To succeed, it's essential to understand who your customers are, how they interact with your online store, and what factors influence their buying decisions. This is where Google Analytics and Meta Pixel (formerly known as Facebook Pixel) come into play.

Configuring Google Analytics and Meta Pixel is a crucial step in optimizing your Shopify store. These powerful tools allow you to track and analyze visitor behavior on your site. They gather valuable data that provides insights into who your customers are, how they navigate your site, which products they view, and, most importantly, what motivates them to make a purchase.

This information is essential for improving your store and increasing your sales. For example, by understanding which products are the most popular, you can feature these items on your homepage to attract more customers. Similarly, by analyzing your customers' navigation paths, you can identify potential conversion obstacles and work to eliminate them to streamline the purchasing process.

But that's not all; Google Analytics and Meta Pixel also offer advanced features like conversion tracking and retargeting, which can help you refine your marketing strategy and reach your customers more effectively.

In this chapter, we will guide you through the steps to set up Google Analytics and Meta Pixel for your Shopify store. We will cover everything from creating your account to configuring tracking events. So, get ready to dive into the fascinating world of data analysis and discover how these tools can propel your Shopify store to new heights.

1. Google Analytics Setup

a. Creating a Google Analytics Account

Before you can delve into the rich and detailed world of your website's data, the first step is to create a Google Analytics account if you don't already have one. Google Analytics is a free service that allows you to track website traffic and analyze visitor behavior.

To create an account, visit the Google Analytics website. You will be greeted by a user-friendly interface that will guide you through the account creation process. You'll need to provide some basic information, such as your email address and the name of your business. You'll also need to accept Google Analytics' terms of use.

Once you've created your account, Google will provide you with a unique tracking ID. This ID is crucial because it links your website to your Google Analytics account and enables data tracking. You'll need to copy this tracking ID and paste it into your Shopify store settings, but we'll cover this step in more detail later.

Creating a Google Analytics account is a simple yet crucial step to understanding and optimizing visitor behavior on your Shopify store. With your account in place, you'll be ready to start collecting data and using that information to improve your store and increase your sales.

b. Adding Your Shopify Store to Google Analytics

Once you've created your Google Analytics account, the next step is to add your Shopify store to Google Analytics. This step is essential because it allows Google Analytics to start collecting data on visitor behavior on your store.

To add your Shopify store to Google Analytics, you'll need to copy your Google Analytics tracking ID. This tracking ID is a unique numerical code that identifies your Google Analytics account. You can find it in the settings of your Google Analytics account under "Tracking Information."

After copying your tracking ID, log in to your Shopify account and go to the "Online Store" section of your settings. Here, you'll find a field titled "Google Analytics." Paste your tracking ID into this field and click "Save."

By adding your Shopify store to Google Analytics, you enable Google to start collecting data on visitor behavior on your store. This data can provide valuable insights into what actions users take after visiting your store, which products they view, and the transactions they make. This information can help you improve your store, optimize your marketing strategy, and ultimately increase your sales.

c. Enabling E-commerce Tracking

E-commerce tracking is a powerful feature of Google Analytics that allows you to track and analyze sales and transactions on your Shopify store. By enabling this feature, you can get detailed insights into the products your customers are purchasing, the number of transactions made, the revenue generated from these transactions, and more.

To activate e-commerce tracking, you need to access the settings of your Google Analytics account. Once in your settings, look for the "Tracking Info" section. Under this section, you'll find an option called "E-commerce Settings." Click on this option to enable e-commerce tracking.

After enabling e-commerce tracking, Google Analytics will start collecting data on sales and transactions on your Shopify store. This data can provide valuable insights into which products are most popular, customer buying behaviors, and how you can optimize your store to increase sales and revenue.

It's important to note that e-commerce tracking doesn't start immediately after activation. It may take some time before Google Analytics begins collecting data. However, once the data starts flowing, you'll have access to a wealth of information that can help you improve your store and boost your sales.

d. Setting Up Goals

Goals in Google Analytics are specific actions you want visitors to your site to take. These actions can be as simple as visiting a particular page or as complex as purchasing a product. By configuring goals, you can track these actions and gain valuable insights into user behavior on your site.

To set up goals, you'll need to access the settings of your Google Analytics account. Once in your settings, look for the "Goals" section. Here, you can create new goals by clicking the "+ New Goal" button.

When creating a goal, you'll need to provide certain information. First, you'll need to give your goal a name that clearly describes the action you want to track. Next, you'll need to choose the goal type. Google Analytics offers several goal types, including destination (e.g., a visitor reaches a specific page), duration (e.g., a visitor spends a certain amount of time on your site), pages/screens per session (e.g., a visitor views a certain number of pages), and event (e.g., a visitor performs a specific action like purchasing a product).

Once you've chosen the goal type, you'll need to configure the goal details. For example, if you choose a destination goal, you'll need to provide the URL of the page you want visitors to reach. If you choose an event goal, you'll need to provide details about the event you want to track.

Configuring goals in Google Analytics may seem complex, but it's essential for understanding user behavior on your site. By tracking specific actions you want users to take, you can gain valuable insights that can help you optimize your store, fine-tune your advertising campaigns, and ultimately increase your sales.

2. Meta Pixel Setup

a. Creating a Meta Pixel

The Meta Pixel, formerly known as Facebook Pixel, is a tracking tool that allows you to measure the effectiveness of your ads, understand the actions people take on your website, and target your ads more precisely. The first step in using the Meta Pixel is to create it in the Events Manager of your Facebook Ads Manager account.

To create a Meta Pixel, log in to your Facebook Ads Manager account. Once logged in, navigate to the "Measure & Report" menu and select "Events Manager." In the Events Manager, you'll see an option to "Connect Data Sources." Click on this option and choose "Web" from the available data source options, including the Meta Pixel.

Once you've selected the Meta Pixel, you'll be guided through the process of creating the pixel. You'll need to give your pixel a name, which can be helpful if you manage multiple pixels. Try to choose a name that reflects the intended use of this pixel, such as "Shopify Store Pixel."

Next, you'll need to enter the URL of your website. This allows Facebook to verify that the pixel can be correctly installed on your site. After entering this information, click "Continue" to create your Meta Pixel.

Creating a Meta Pixel is a crucial step to make the most of your Facebook marketing efforts. With a Meta Pixel in place, you can track the actions people take on your site after seeing your Facebook ads. You can use this information to refine your ads and target your audience more effectively.

b. Adding Your Meta Pixel to Your Shopify Store

Once you've created your Meta Pixel, the next step is to integrate it into your Shopify store. This is a critical step that allows Meta to start collecting data on user interactions with your store. This data can be used to optimize your advertising campaigns, improve ad targeting, and increase the effectiveness of your marketing efforts.

To add your Meta Pixel to your Shopify store, you first need to copy the ID of your Pixel. You can find this ID in the Events Manager of your Facebook Ads Manager account. It's a unique numerical code that identifies your Meta Pixel.

After copying the Pixel ID, log in to your Shopify account. In your Shopify dashboard, navigate to the "Preferences" section within your store settings. Here, you'll find a section titled "Facebook Pixel." Paste your Pixel ID into the corresponding field and click "Save."

By adding your Meta Pixel to your Shopify store, you enable Meta to start collecting data on user behavior within your store. This data can provide valuable insights into the actions users take after seeing your ads, the products they view, and the transactions they complete. This information can be used to refine your advertising campaigns, improve ad targeting, and ultimately maximize the return on investment of your marketing efforts.

c. Configuring Events

Events, in the context of the Meta Pixel, are specific actions that visitors take on your website. These actions can range from visiting a specific page to adding a product to the cart or making a purchase. By configuring events, you can track these actions and gain valuable insights into user behavior on your site.

To configure events, you need to access the Events Manager in your Facebook Ads Manager account. In the Events Manager, you'll find a section called "Data Sources." This is where you can see all your Meta Pixels and configure events for each of them.

When setting up an event, you first need to choose the type of event you want to track. Meta offers a variety of predefined events you can choose from, such as "View Content," "Add to Cart," "Purchase," and many more. Each event corresponds to a specific action users can take on your site.

Once you've selected the event type, you'll need to configure event details. For example, if you choose the "View Content" event, you'll specify which content you want to track, such as a specific product page or a product category.

Configuring events in the Meta Pixel may appear complex, but it's essential for understanding user behavior on your site. By tracking specific actions you want users to take, you can gain valuable insights that can help you optimize your store, fine-tune your advertising campaigns, and ultimately increase your sales.

d. Using Pixel for Retargeting

Retargeting is a powerful marketing strategy that allows you to show ads to people who have previously visited your site or interacted with your products. It's an effective way to remind visitors of products they've viewed or added to their cart and encourage them to return to your site to make a purchase. The Meta Pixel plays a crucial role in retargeting by allowing you to track site visitors and target ads based on their behavior.

To use the Meta Pixel for retargeting, you first need to set up retargeting events in the Events Manager of your Facebook Ads Manager account. These events can include actions like visiting a product page, adding a product to the cart, or signing up for a newsletter.

Once you've configured your retargeting events, you can create custom audiences based on these events. For example, you can create an audience of people who added a product to their cart but didn't complete a purchase. You can then target your ads to this audience to encourage them to return to your site and complete their purchase.

In addition to creating audiences based on specific events, you can also use the Meta Pixel to create lookalike audiences. These audiences are composed of people who share similar characteristics with your existing audience, allowing you to expand your reach and attract new potential customers.

Using the Meta Pixel for retargeting can significantly improve the effectiveness of your advertising campaigns. By targeting ads to people who have already shown interest in your products, you can increase your chances of conversion and maximize the return on investment of your marketing efforts.

3. Conclusion

Configuring Google Analytics and Meta Pixel is much more than a technical step in setting up your Shopify store. It's a strategic approach that opens the doors to a deep understanding of your customers and their behaviors. These tools provide you with valuable data that can transform how you manage your store and interact with your customers.

By analyzing visitor behavior on your site, you can discover trends, identify opportunities, and spot potential issues. This information can help you improve the user experience on your store, optimize your products and pages, and increase your sales.

Furthermore, Google Analytics and Meta Pixel offer you the ability to track the effectiveness of your marketing efforts. Whether you're launching a new advertising campaign or testing different SEO strategies, these tools can provide you with valuable insights that can help you refine your efforts and maximize your return on investment.

By following the steps outlined in this chapter, you can set up Google Analytics and Meta Pixel for your Shopify store. However, configuring these tools is just the beginning. To fully harness their benefits, you need to regularly analyze the data they provide, test different strategies, and adjust your efforts based on the results.

In the end, Google Analytics and Meta Pixel are powerful tools that can help you understand your customers, improve your store, and increase your sales. By using them strategically, you can transform your Shopify store into a thriving and profitable e-commerce business.

CHAPTER 11: HOW TO CREATE A MARKETING STRATEGY FOR YOUR SHOPIFY STORE

1. Step 1: Situation Analysis

Before you can develop an effective marketing strategy, you need to understand your current situation. This step, often referred to as SWOT analysis (Strengths, Weaknesses, Opportunities, Threats), allows you to assess your strengths, weaknesses, available opportunities, and potential threats.

a. Target Market Analysis

Understanding who your potential customers are is crucial. What are their ages, interests, buying behaviors? What types of products are they looking for? What are their needs and desires? This understanding will help you target your marketing efforts more effectively.

b. Competitive Analysis

In the world of dropshipping, competition can be fierce. Who are your main competitors? What products do they offer? How do they market their products? What are their strengths and weaknesses? A thorough analysis of the competition can help you identify opportunities to stand out.

c. Evaluation of Your Own Strengths and Weaknesses

As a Shopify store, what are your strengths? Perhaps you have an excellent product selection, exceptional customer service, or expertise in your niche. On the other hand, what are your weaknesses? Maybe you struggle to generate traffic to your store, or perhaps your conversion rate could be improved. An honest evaluation of your strengths and weaknesses can help you determine where to focus your marketing efforts.

d. Examination of External Factors

Finally, it's important to consider any external factors that could affect your business. This could include market trends, regulatory changes, technological advancements, or even global events. For example, the COVID-19 pandemic had a significant impact on e-commerce, with an increase in online shopping and changes in consumer buying behavior.

In summary, situation analysis is a crucial step in developing your marketing strategy. It gives you an overview of your current position and helps you identify the opportunities and challenges you may encounter.

2. Step 2: Define Your Target Audience

Defining your target audience is a crucial step in developing your marketing strategy. In the context of dropshipping, this means understanding who your ideal customers are, what products they are looking for, how they prefer to shop online, and how you can reach them effectively.

a. Identifying Ideal Customers

Your ideal customers are those most likely to be interested in the products you offer. They can be defined based on various criteria, such as age, gender, geographic location, interests, buying behavior, and more. For example, if you sell sports apparel, your target audience could be people interested in fitness and wellness.

b. Understanding Customer Needs and Desires

What types of products are your customers looking for? What are their needs and desires? Understanding this can help you select the right products to sell, define your marketing messages, and create a shopping experience that meets your customers' expectations.

c. Understanding Online Shopping Habits

How does your target audience like to shop online? Do they prefer to buy on e-commerce platforms like Amazon, or do they prefer to buy directly from brand websites? What types of payment methods do they prefer? What factors influence their purchase decisions (e.g., customer reviews, free shipping, promotions)? Understanding these habits can help you optimize your Shopify store to cater to your customers' preferences.

d. Reaching Your Target Audience

Finally, how can you effectively reach your target audience? Which marketing channels are they most likely to use? What types of messages are they likely to respond to? For example, if your target audience is young and tech-savvy, you may find that social media is an effective marketing channel.

In summary, defining your target audience allows you to understand who your customers are, what they want, and how you can reach them. This allows you to focus your marketing efforts on people most likely to be interested in your products, which can increase the effectiveness of your marketing and improve return on investment.

3. Step 3: Establish Your Marketing Goals

Every marketing initiative you undertake should be guided by specific, measurable goals. These goals can be short-term or long-term and may aim to attract new customers, retain existing customers, or increase sales of a particular product in your Shopify store.

a. Short-Term Goals

Short-term goals typically focus on immediate sales growth

and may include objectives such as increasing website traffic, improving conversion rates, or boosting sales of a specific product. These goals are often measured over a period of a few weeks to a few months.

b. Long-Term Goals

Long-term goals generally focus on the growth and sustainability of your business. They may include objectives such as expanding your product range, entering new markets, or increasing customer lifetime value. These goals are often measured over several months to several years.

c. Attracting New Customers

One of the most common goals for dropshipping businesses is to attract new customers. This may involve strategies such as SEO, paid advertising, social media marketing, and more.

d. Retaining Existing Customers

It is often more cost-effective to retain existing customers than to acquire new ones. You can aim to increase purchase frequency, average order value, or customer retention rates.

e. Increasing Sales of a Specific Product

If you have a product that performs particularly well or one that you want to promote, you can set specific marketing goals to increase sales of that product.

In summary, establishing clear and measurable marketing goals is an essential step in developing your marketing strategy. These goals provide you with a clear direction and allow you to measure the effectiveness of your marketing efforts.

4. Step 4: Choose Your Marketing Channels

There are many marketing channels you can use to promote your dropshipping Shopify store. The choice of channels to use will depend on your goals, target audience, and budget. Here is a more detailed description of some popular marketing channels.

a. Paid Advertising

Paid advertising, such as Google Ads or Facebook Ads, can be an effective way to quickly attract traffic to your store. However, it can also be expensive, especially in a highly competitive niche. It's important to carefully monitor the return on investment of your paid advertising to ensure it's profitable.

b. Content Marketing

Content marketing, such as writing blog articles or creating videos, can be an effective way to attract visitors to your store and convert them into customers. Content marketing can also help improve your SEO, increasing your visibility on search engines.

c. Social Media

Social media platforms like Facebook, Instagram, and Twitter can be effective marketing channels, especially if your target audience is active on these platforms. You can use social media to promote your products, engage with your audience, and even provide customer service.

d. Email Marketing

Email marketing can be a cost-effective way to retain and engage your customers. You can use email to inform customers about new products, offer special promotions, and more. It's important to ensure that your emails provide value to your customers to prevent them from unsubscribing.

e. Partnerships and Collaborations

Working with other brands or influencers can be an effective way to reach a broader audience. This could involve sponsored social media posts, product collaborations, or joint events.

In summary, the choice of your marketing channels will depend on many factors, including your goals, target audience, and budget. It's important to test different channels to see which ones are most effective for your business.

5. Step 5: Impact Analysis

Once you have implemented your marketing strategy, it's important to analyze its impact. This analysis will help you understand if your marketing efforts are effective, where you can make improvements, and how you can optimize your marketing initiatives for better results.

a. Tracking Key Performance Indicators (KPIs)

Key Performance Indicators (KPIs) are quantitative measures that help you assess the effectiveness of your marketing efforts. This can include measures such as website traffic, conversion rate, cost per acquisition, customer lifetime value, and more. It's important to choose KPIs that are directly related to your marketing goals.

b. Data Analysis

Analyzing the data from your Shopify store and marketing campaigns can provide valuable insights into the effectiveness of your efforts. For example, you can analyze Google Analytics data to understand how visitors interact with your website or review data from your advertising campaigns to determine which messages are most effective.

c. A/B Testing

A/B testing can be an effective way to optimize your marketing efforts. This involves testing two different versions of a marketing element (such as a product page, an ad, or an email) to see which one is more effective.

d. Customer Feedback

Customer feedback can be a valuable source of information about the effectiveness of your marketing. You can collect feedback through surveys, social media comments, or by directly asking your customers for their opinions.

In summary, analyzing the impact of your marketing is an essential step in optimizing your efforts and achieving better results. By tracking KPIs, analyzing data, conducting A/B tests, and listening to customer feedback, you can continually improve your marketing and achieve your business goals.

6. Step 6: Review and Adjustment

Creating a marketing strategy for your dropshipping Shopify store is not a one-time process but an ongoing effort. As your business evolves, your marketing tactics will need to evolve as well. Therefore, it's important to regularly review your marketing strategy and make necessary adjustments.

a. Regular Review

It is recommended to review your marketing strategy at least once a quarter. This allows you to take into account changes in your business, market, or competitive environment. For example, if you launch a new product, you may need to adjust your marketing strategy to promote it.

b. Adjustment Based on Results

When reviewing your marketing strategy, it's essential to consider the results of your previous marketing efforts. If certain tactics are not producing the desired results, it may be necessary to adjust or abandon them. Similarly, if certain tactics are particularly effective, you may want to allocate more resources to them.

c. Experimentation and Innovation

The marketing landscape is constantly evolving, with new tactics and technologies emerging regularly. Therefore, it's essential to remain open to experimentation and innovation. This could involve trying out new social media platforms, experimenting with augmented reality or virtual reality, or testing new content or storytelling approaches.

d. Training and Continuous Learning

To stay up-to-date with the latest marketing trends and tactics, it's important to engage in continuous learning and training. This may involve taking online courses, attending conferences or webinars, or reading books and blogs on marketing.

In summary, reviewing and adjusting your marketing strategy are essential steps to ensure the ongoing success of your dropshipping Shopify store. By staying flexible and responsive, you can ensure that your marketing remains effective and aligned with your business goals.

By following these steps, you can create an effective marketing strategy that will help you achieve your business goals and thrive in the world of dropshipping with Shopify.

CHAPTER 12: HOW TO USE EMAIL MARKETING AND SOCIAL MEDIA MARKETING FOR YOUR SHOPIFY STORE

In the dynamic world of e-commerce, visibility and customer engagement are two key elements of success. For a Shopify store, this means not only having a strong online presence but also knowing how to effectively use the digital marketing tools at your disposal. Among these tools, email marketing and social media marketing stand out as powerful strategies to reach and engage your target audience.

Email marketing, a proven and effective method, allows you to reach your customers directly in their inbox, providing a personal platform to share updates, promotions, and personalized content. On the other hand, social media marketing offers a dynamic platform to reach a wide audience, boost engagement, and build a community around your brand.

However, the effective use of these tools requires more than just promotional messages or random posts. It requires a well-thought-out strategy, a clear understanding of your target audience, and in-depth knowledge of best practices and current trends.

In this chapter, we will delve into the world of email marketing and social media marketing. We will explore how you can strategically use these channels to increase the visibility of your Shopify store, attract and retain more customers, and ultimately, boost your sales. Whether you're a digital marketing beginner or looking to refine your existing strategies, this chapter will provide you with valuable insights and practical tips for success.

◆ ◆ ◆

1. Email Marketing for Your Shopify Store

Email marketing is a powerful communication tool that offers a direct and personal connection with your customers. Unlike other forms of digital marketing that rely on the algorithm of a third-party platform, email marketing gives you full control over your message and its distribution. It's a channel that allows you to speak directly to your customers in a space they regularly check - their inbox.

One of the major advantages of email marketing is its versatility. Whether you're launching a new product, announcing a flash sale, sharing company news, or providing helpful tips, email marketing can be adapted to meet a variety of objectives. Moreover, with the ability to segment your email list, you can customize your messages to address the specific needs and interests of different customer groups.

Email marketing is also a valuable tool for building customer loyalty. By offering valuable content and exclusive offers to your email subscribers, you can not only encourage repeat purchases but also strengthen the relationship between your customers and your brand. This can lead to greater brand loyalty, higher retention rates, and higher customer lifetime value.

Finally, email marketing offers an impressive return on investment. In fact, according to a study by the Direct Marketing Association, email marketing can deliver a return on investment of up to 4300%. This makes email marketing a cost-effective strategy for Shopify stores of all sizes.

In the following sections, we will explore how you can establish an effective email marketing strategy for your Shopify store, from steps to create an email list to designing engaging and converting email campaigns.

a. Choosing an Email Marketing Service

In today's digital landscape, there are a multitude of email marketing services, each offering a unique range of features, pricing options, and integration capabilities. Some of the most popular services include Mailchimp, SendinBlue, and Klaviyo. Choosing the right service for your Shopify store may seem like a daunting task, but by considering a few key factors, you can make an informed choice that supports your email marketing goals.

One of the most important factors to consider is integration with Shopify. An email marketing service that seamlessly integrates with Shopify can significantly streamline your email marketing workflow. For example, good integration can allow you to automatically sync your customer lists, track purchasing behavior, and personalize your emails based on your store's data.

Next, you should consider the features offered by the email marketing service. This may include tools for email creation, email automation, email list segmentation, analytics and reporting, and more. Make sure to choose a service that offers the features you need to achieve your email marketing objectives.

Cost is another important factor to consider. Email marketing services can vary widely in terms of pricing, with options for every budget. It's important to choose a service that fits your budget, but keep in mind that cost should be balanced with the features and capabilities of the service.

Finally, you should also consider the reputation and reviews of the email marketing service. Reviews from other users can provide valuable insights into the service's reliability, quality of customer support, and overall user satisfaction.

By taking these factors into account, you can choose an email marketing service that supports your marketing goals, seamlessly integrates with your Shopify store, offers the features you need, fits your budget, and has a strong reputation for quality and service.

b. Building an Email List

Building an email list is a fundamental step to get started with email marketing. A strong email list is the backbone of any successful email marketing strategy because it allows you to communicate directly with customers and prospects who have shown an interest in your brand.

The most common way to build an email list is by adding a newsletter signup option on your website. This can be done by adding a simple signup form on your homepage, product pages, or even as a step in the checkout process. Ensure that the signup form is easy to find and use to encourage visitors to subscribe.

However, having a signup form is not enough. It's also important to make the signup option enticing for visitors. This can be done by offering an incentive for signing up, such as a discount on the first purchase, access to exclusive offers, or updates on new products and upcoming sales. You can also use persuasive and engaging language to explain the benefits of subscribing to your newsletter.

In addition to the signup option on your website, you can also consider other methods to grow your email list. For example, you can encourage signups at in-person events, use social media to promote your newsletter, or even offer an email signup option for customers who shop in your physical store.

It's important to note that, regardless of the methods you use to grow your email list, you should always obtain explicit consent from individuals to receive marketing emails from you. This is not only a best practice but also a legal requirement in many countries.

Finally, once you've started building your email list, it's important to maintain it. This means regularly cleaning your list to remove invalid or inactive email addresses and continuing to encourage new signups to keep your email list fresh and relevant.

c. Creating Email Campaigns

With an email list in place, you're ready to start creating email campaigns. Email campaigns are series of emails sent to specific segments of your email list, designed to encourage a certain action or outcome, such as a purchase, engagement, or brand awareness.

The type of email campaign you choose to create will depend on your specific marketing goals. Here are some types of email campaigns you might consider:

i. *New Product Announcements*

If you're launching a new product or collection, an email campaign can be an excellent way to spread the word. You can create an email (or a series of emails) that highlights the product's features, shows the product in action, and encourages recipients to make a purchase.

ii.   Promotions and Sales

Promotional emails are a powerful tool for boosting sales. Whether you're offering a limited-time discount, a special offer for email subscribers, or an end-of-season sale, an email campaign can help increase the visibility of the offer and encourage purchases.

iii.   Educational Content

Emails don't always have to be sales-focused. Sharing helpful tips, product usage guides, or other educational content can help establish your brand as a trusted resource and strengthen the relationship with your customers.

iv.   Company Updates

Emails can also be an effective way to share news or company updates. Whether you're announcing a new hire, sharing a significant milestone, or telling a story about your company's mission, these emails can help strengthen the connection between your brand and your customers.

When creating your email campaigns, it's important to keep a few best practices in mind. First, ensure that each email has a clear objective and a strong call to action. Second, try to personalize your emails as much as possible, whether by using the recipient's name or tailoring the content based on their preferences or purchase behavior. Finally, don't forget to test and optimize your emails based on performance to continuously improve your email campaigns.

2.   Social Media Marketing

for Your Shopify Store

In today's digital era, social media marketing has become an indispensable tool for any business aiming to boost its visibility and reach a wider audience. For a Shopify store, effective use of social media can not only increase brand awareness and drive more traffic to your store but also create an engaged community around your brand.

Social media marketing goes beyond merely posting promotional content. It involves creating and sharing content that resonates with your audience, encourages engagement, and fosters a deeper relationship between your customers and your brand. Whether through product posts, behind-the-scenes videos, interactive contests, or live discussions, each social media interaction provides an opportunity to showcase your brand's personality and enhance customer loyalty.

Moreover, social media platforms provide a space to listen to and interact with your customers. Whether it's responding to comments, addressing customer service issues, or gathering feedback, each interaction is a chance to learn from your customers and improve your offerings.

Additionally, social media can be a powerful tool for targeting and advertising. With detailed targeting options based on demographic data, user interests, and behavior, you can reach a specific audience with your messages and ads, thereby enhancing the effectiveness of your marketing efforts.

However, social media marketing requires a well-thought-out strategy and consistent execution. In the following sections, we will explore how you can choose the right social media platforms for your brand, create engaging content, and use social media advertising to achieve your marketing goals.

a. Choosing the Right Social Media Platforms

With a multitude of social media platforms available today, it can be challenging to determine where to focus your efforts. Each platform has its unique features, audience, and preferred communication methods. Facebook, Instagram, Twitter, Pinterest, and LinkedIn are among the most popular, but there are also other platforms like Snapchat, TikTok, and YouTube that may be relevant depending on your target audience and product type.

To choose the right platforms for your Shopify store, you first need to understand your target audience. How old are they? What are their interests? On which platforms do they spend the most time? For example, if you target a younger audience, platforms like Instagram and TikTok may be more relevant. If you sell visually appealing products like clothing or jewelry, Pinterest and Instagram could be good choices.

Next, consider the type of content you can create and regularly share. Instagram and Pinterest are heavily image-focused, while Twitter is ideal for quick updates and content sharing. Facebook and LinkedIn are excellent for sharing a variety of content, including blog articles, company updates, and more.

It's also essential to take into account the resources at your disposal. Managing multiple social media accounts can be time-consuming, so it's better to focus on a few platforms and excel on them rather than spreading yourself too thin.

Lastly, remember that platform choice is a decision that should be regularly reassessed. Social media trends change rapidly, and what works today may not work tomorrow. Keep an eye on the performance of your social media marketing efforts and don't hesitate to adjust your strategy if needed.

b. Creating Engaging Content

On social media, content is more than just king—it is the heart and soul of your online presence. Quality content can help grab attention, spark interest, encourage engagement, and build a lasting relationship with your audience. That's why it's crucial to create content that is not only interesting and relevant to your brand but also encourages users to interact and engage.

i. Product Photos

High-quality images of your products can be incredibly effective on visual platforms like Instagram and Pinterest. Try to capture your products from different angles, in context, and in action to show potential customers what to expect.

ii. Videos

Videos are increasingly popular on social media and can be an excellent way to showcase your products in action, share tutorials or product demonstrations, or even provide a behind-the-scenes look at your business.

iii. Blog Posts

If you have a blog, sharing your articles on social media can help drive traffic to your website. Ensure your articles are relevant and valuable to your target audience.

iv. Contests and Giveaways

Contests and giveaways can be a great way to encourage engagement and gain new subscribers. Make sure the rules are clear, and the prize is enticing to your target audience.

v. User-Generated Content

Encouraging your followers to share their photos or experiences with your products can not only provide authentic content for your brand but also build trust and customer loyalty.

vi. Stories and Live Updates

Features like Instagram Stories and Facebook Live offer unique ways to share real-time content with your audience, whether it's a product announcement, a live event, or a typical day at your business.

When creating content, always keep your target audience and brand goals in mind. Ensure your content aligns with your brand and adds value to your subscribers. And remember, engagement is a two-way street—be sure to respond to comments, thank subscribers for their support, and interact with your community authentically and personally.

c. Using Social Media Advertising

Social media advertising is a powerful tool that can help amplify your reach, attract a broader audience, and boost conversions for your Shopify store. With precise targeting options and a variety of ad formats, social media ads can be an effective complement to your organic marketing strategy.

Each social media platform offers its own advertising tools, each with its own advantages:

i. Facebook Ads

Facebook offers a range of ad formats, including video ads, product carousels, and sponsored posts. With detailed targeting options based on age, gender, location, interests, and behavior, you can reach the right audience with the right message.

ii. Instagram Ads

Since Instagram is owned by Facebook, you can use the same targeting tools to create visually appealing ads in Instagram's feed or Stories.

iii. *Twitter Ads*

Twitter offers options to promote individual tweets, increase brand awareness, or drive website traffic. Targeting can be based on keywords, interests, geographical locations, and more.

iv. *Pinterest Ads*

If you sell visually appealing products, Pinterest can be an excellent platform for advertising. Ads appear like regular pins but are marked as sponsored.

v. *LinkedIn Ads*

If you sell B2B products or want to reach professionals in a specific industry, LinkedIn can be an excellent option. Ads can be targeted based on industry, job position, experience level, and more.

When creating social media ads, it's important to keep a few best practices in mind. First, ensure that your ads align with your brand and marketing goals. Second, use targeting to reach the right audience with the right message. Finally, test and optimize your ads based on performance to maximize your return on investment.

By using social media advertising strategically, you can increase the visibility of your Shopify store, attract more potential customers, and boost sales.

3. Conclusion

Email marketing and social media marketing are much more than mere promotional tools—they are essential communication channels that can help you build a strong relationship with your audience, increase the visibility of your Shopify store, and boost sales.

Email marketing allows you to communicate directly with your customers on a regular basis, providing them with timely and relevant information about your products, offers, and brand. With a well-thought-out email marketing strategy, you can not only attract new customers but also retain existing customers and encourage repeat purchases.

On the other hand, social media marketing provides you with a platform to tell your brand's story, share engaging content, and interact with your audience in a more informal and personal manner. By using social media to create a community around your brand, you can increase engagement, strengthen brand loyalty, and transform your subscribers into brand ambassadors.

However, it's important to remember that success in email marketing and social media marketing doesn't happen overnight. It requires a well-planned strategy, consistent execution, and a willingness to experiment, learn, and optimize based on performance. But with time, effort, and perseverance, these tools can play a key role in the growth of your Shopify store.

In the end, email marketing and social media marketing are two essential pieces of the digital marketing puzzle. By using them effectively and integrating them into a broader marketing strategy, you can create a consistent and engaging brand experience that attracts and retains customers.

CHAPTER 13: HOW TO USE INFLUENCER MARKETING AND PAID ADVERTISING FOR YOUR SHOPIFY STORE

In the world of e-commerce, competition is fierce. To stand out and attract customers, it's essential to use effective marketing strategies. Two of the most powerful strategies are influencer marketing and paid advertising. In this chapter, we will explore how you can use these two strategies to increase the visibility of your Shopify store and boost your sales.

❖ ❖ ❖

1. *Section 1: Influencer Marketing*

Influencer marketing is a marketing strategy that has gained traction with the rise of social media. It involves using the persuasive power of certain individuals, known as influencers, to promote products or services.
Influencers are individuals who have succeeded in building a following on social media. They can be content creators, celebrities, athletes, artists, bloggers, experts in a specific field,

and more. What they have in common is a strong online presence and the ability to influence the purchasing decisions of their community through their expertise, authenticity, and closeness to their audience.

Influencers have a trusted relationship with their community. Their followers respect and value their opinions. They are often perceived as thought leaders and sources of inspiration. Therefore, when an influencer recommends a product or service, their followers are more likely to view it favorably.

What interests brands in influencer marketing is the influencer's ability to reach and engage a specific audience. By working with influencers, brands can reach a targeted and engaged audience, which can lead to increased brand awareness, engagement, and sales.

Influencer marketing is particularly effective because it allows brands to bypass the growing consumer skepticism toward traditional advertising. Consumers are becoming increasingly wary of ads and are more likely to trust a recommendation from an influencer they follow and respect.

In summary, influencer marketing is a powerful strategy that allows brands to connect with consumers in a more personal and authentic way. By working with influencers who align with their brand and target audience, brands can create more effective and engaging marketing campaigns.

a. How to Implement an Influencer Marketing Strategy

Before diving into influencer marketing, it's crucial to clearly define your goals. This is the first step in creating an effective influencer marketing strategy. Are you looking to increase brand visibility, boost sales, enhance your brand image, or perhaps a combination of these?

If your goal is to grow and increase your brand's visibility, influencer marketing can be an excellent way to achieve that. Influencers already have an engaged audience that trusts them. When they share content about your brand, it can help increase your visibility and attract new customers.

Moreover, influencer marketing can offer a much higher return on investment (ROI) than traditional advertising. According to several industry players, the ROI in influencer marketing is around €7 for every €1 invested, which is significantly higher than other practices like Facebook advertising. This is because influencer recommendations are often perceived as more authentic and credible than traditional ads.

Here are some steps to implement an influencer marketing strategy:

i. *Define your goals*

The first step is to define what you want to achieve with influencer marketing. Your goals may include increasing brand awareness, boosting sales, improving brand image, and more.

ii. *Create an "Instagrammable" product/brand*

Your product or brand should be attractive and interesting to be shared on social media. This increases the likelihood of influencers agreeing to work with you, and their followers being interested in your product or service.

iii. *Identify your target audience*

Who are the people you're trying to reach with your influencer marketing campaign? Understanding your target audience will help you choose the right influencers for your campaign.

iv. *Choose the right influencers*

Not all influencers are created equal. Some may have a large audience, but if that audience isn't relevant to your brand, their influence won't be effective. It's important to select influencers with an audience that matches your target audience and has a brand image that aligns with yours.

v. Create a marketing offer and brief

Clearly define what you expect from the influencer and what you're willing to offer in return. This could include details on the type of content you want them to create, how often you want them to post, and more.

vi. Calculate the influencer marketing budget

How much are you willing to spend on your influencer marketing campaign? Keep in mind that some influencers may charge high fees for their collaboration. It's important to establish a realistic budget that allows you to achieve your goals without breaking the bank.

vii. Reach out to influencers

Once you've identified the influencers you want to work with, you'll need to make them a collaboration proposal. This could include details on what you expect from them, what you're willing to offer in return, and more.

viii. Choose an influencer

Based on your discussions with influencers, choose the one that best fits your needs and budget.

ix. Create a contract with the influencer

Once you've chosen an influencer, establish a contract that outlines the expectations of each party. This may include details on the type of content to create, the publishing schedule, compensation, and more.

x.   *Track and measure results*

Finally, it's important to track and measure the results of your influencer marketing campaign. This will help you understand what's working, what's not, and how you can improve your future campaigns. Use analytics tools to monitor the performance of your campaigns and adjust your strategy accordingly.

b. Working with an Influencer Agency

If you feel overwhelmed by the process of setting up an influencer marketing campaign, or if you simply don't have the time to manage all the details, working with an influencer agency can be an excellent option.

An influencer agency is a company specialized in connecting brands with the right influencers. They typically have an extensive network of influencers in various fields and can help you find those that best match your brand and target audience.

In addition to helping you find the right influencers, an agency can also assist you in negotiating contracts. This may include determining the type of content to create, the number of posts, influencer compensation, and more. Agencies usually have a good understanding of market rates and can help you get the best return on investment.

An agency can also manage the campaign for you. This may include coordinating with the influencer, tracking posts, measuring results, and adjusting the campaign based on performance. This can save you a lot of time and allow you to focus on other aspects of your business.

Finally, an influencer agency can provide you with detailed reports on the performance of your campaign. This may include information on the number of views, likes, shares, comments, engagement rate, traffic generated to your website, sales generated, and more. This information can be valuable for understanding the effectiveness of your campaign and planning your future influencer marketing initiatives.

However, it's important to note that working with an influencer agency can be costly. Agency fees are in addition to influencer compensation costs. Therefore, it's important to understand the associated costs before deciding to work with an agency.

2. Section 2: Paid Advertising

Paid advertising, also known as online advertising or paid digital marketing, is an effective way to generate traffic to your Shopify store. It involves purchasing advertising space on various online platforms to promote your brand, products, or services.

One of the primary advantages of paid advertising is its ability to quickly reach a broad audience. Additionally, most advertising platforms offer detailed targeting options, allowing you to precisely target your audience based on criteria such as age, gender, location, interests, buying behavior, and more. This can enhance the effectiveness of your ads and maximize your return on investment (ROI).

There are many advertising platforms available to reach your target audience. Each has its own advantages and disadvantages, and the best one for you will depend on your target audience, goals, and budget. Here are some of the most popular paid advertising platforms:

a. Facebook & Instagram Ads

These two platforms are integrated, allowing you to create ads that will run on both. Facebook and Instagram offer a variety of targeting options, including age, gender, location, interests, and more. You can also create dynamic product ads that automatically display products to people who have visited your website. Moreover, these platforms provide various ad formats, from simple images and videos to carousels and interactive stories, allowing you to engage your audience creatively.

b. Google & YouTube Ads

Google offers a variety of advertising options, including search ads, display ads, shopping ads, and video ads on YouTube. Google Ads allows you to target users based on their searches, interests, location, and more. YouTube ads, in particular, can be an excellent way to showcase your products visually and engagingly, leveraging the growing popularity of video content.

c. Pinterest Ads

Pinterest is a visual platform where users discover new ideas and products. Pinterest ads can be an effective way to present your products to an engaged audience. Pinterest users often seek inspiration and are more likely to be receptive to new brands and products.

d. Snapchat Ads

Snapchat is a popular platform among young users. Snapchat ads can be an effective way to reach this audience. Snapchat offers unique ad formats, such as sponsored filters and stories, which can increase brand awareness and engagement.

e. Simprosys Google Shopping Feed

This application helps you submit your product feed to Google Shopping, Facebook Ads, and Microsoft Ads. It automates the process of updating your product ads, ensuring that your ads always have the latest information from your Shopify store.

f. Flexify: Facebook Product Feed

This application helps you sync your product catalog with Facebook to create dynamic product ads. It simplifies managing your product ads on Facebook, automatically updating your ads based on changes in your Shopify store.

Each advertising platform has its advantages and disadvantages. The most suitable platform for you depends on your target audience, budget, and advertising goals. It's recommended to test different platforms and ad types to determine what works best for your Shopify store. Additionally, it's crucial to monitor and analyze the performance of your ads to understand what's effective and what needs adjustment to fine-tune your advertising strategy.

g. Paid Advertising Strategy

i. *Define Your Goals*

Before you start creating ads, it's essential to define what you hope to achieve. Your goals could include increasing brand awareness, driving more traffic to your website, generating sales, and more.

ii. *Determine Your Budget*

Determining your budget is a crucial step in setting up your paid advertising strategy. How much are you willing to invest in achieving your goals? It's important to note that paid advertising often involves testing and learning. You may need to adjust your budget based on the results you're getting. It's recommended to start with a modest budget and gradually increase it as you see the performance of your ads.

iii.   Target Your Audience

Defining your target audience is another critical step. Whom do you want to reach with your ads? Use the targeting options provided by different advertising platforms to reach your ideal audience. This may include targeting by age, gender, location, interests, behaviors, and more. A good understanding of your target audience can help you create more relevant and effective ads.

iv.   Create Compelling Ads

Creating engaging ads is essential to capturing the attention of your target audience. Your ads should stand out and encourage people to click. Use high-quality images, catchy headlines, and persuasive copy to attract your audience. Don't forget to include a clear call to action to guide users to the next step, whether it's purchasing a product, signing up for a newsletter, or something else.

v.   Track and Optimize

Once your ads are running, it's crucial to monitor their performance and optimize accordingly. Use the analytics tools provided by advertising platforms to see which ads are performing the best. Look at key performance indicators such as cost per click (CPC), click-through rate (CTR), return on ad spend (ROAS), and more. Make adjustments based on this information to improve the effectiveness of your ads.

By combining influencer marketing and paid advertising, you

can create a powerful marketing strategy for your Shopify store. These two strategies can complement each other and help you reach a broader audience, increase brand awareness, and boost sales for your Shopify store.

3. Conclusion

Influencer marketing and paid advertising are two essential pillars in the arsenal of any successful digital marketing strategy. When used effectively and strategically, they can significantly contribute to increasing the visibility of your Shopify store, attracting a wider audience, and boosting sales.

In particular, influencer marketing can help establish trust and credibility for your brand by leveraging the reach and influence of respected thought leaders in your industry. Influencers can act as brand ambassadors, presenting your products authentically and engagingly.

On the other hand, paid advertising allows you to precisely target your ideal audience, delivering relevant and compelling ad messages on platforms where they spend their time. Whether it's on search engines like Google, social networks like Facebook and Instagram, or other popular platforms like Pinterest and Snapchat, paid advertising can help you reach potential customers where they are.

However, it's essential to recognize that these strategies are not a magic solution. They require careful planning, meticulous execution, and ongoing optimization to achieve the best results. It's also crucial to track and analyze the performance of your campaigns to understand what's working and what's not, and to make necessary adjustments.

Ultimately, the success of your Shopify store will depend on your ability to use these tools effectively to achieve your marketing goals. By combining influencer marketing and paid advertising and tailoring them to your specific needs, you can create a robust marketing strategy that helps you convert more visitors into loyal customers.

CHAPTER 14: PROVIDING EXCELLENT CUSTOMER SERVICE IN YOUR SHOPIFY STORE

Customer service is the heartbeat of any e-commerce business, and Shopify stores are no exception to this rule. It encompasses all the interactions you have with your customers at every stage of their buying journey - before they place an order, while they browse and make their purchases, and long after they've received their products.

Before the purchase, customer service can take the form of answering questions about your products, helping with site navigation, or providing advice to assist customers in finding the product that best suits their needs. During the purchase, excellent customer service can mean an easy-to-understand ordering process, flexible payment options, and quick responses to any questions or concerns that may arise. After the purchase, customer service continues with order tracking, handling returns and exchanges, and listening to customer feedback to continuously improve your offering.

Excellent customer service is more than just a courtesy - it's a powerful tool that can help retain customers, boost sales, and enhance your brand's reputation. Customers who have positive experiences with your customer service are more likely to make repeat purchases, recommend your store to friends and family, and leave positive reviews that can attract new customers. In other words, excellent customer service can be a growth engine for your Shopify store.

◆ ◆ ◆

1. Understanding Customer Expectations

In today's digital world, customer expectations for customer service are higher than ever. Customers expect service that is not only fast and efficient but also personalized and accessible.

Speed is crucial in customer service. In our connected world where everything is instant, customers expect quick answers to their questions and concerns. Whether it's a product question, a return request, or a complaint, customers want a fast resolution to their issues.

Efficiency is also critical. Customers don't just want quick responses; they also want responses that solve their problems. This means that your customer service team needs to be well-trained and knowledgeable about your products and policies to provide accurate and helpful answers.

Personalization is another key customer expectation. Customers want to feel valued and recognized. They appreciate it when businesses remember their preferences, anticipate their needs, and offer solutions tailored to their specific situations.

Accessibility is a major customer expectation today. Customers want to be able to contact your store through their preferred channel, whether it's email, live chat, social media, or phone. Furthermore, they expect these channels to be available at all times, as today's customers shop and need assistance around the clock.

By understanding these expectations, you can structure your customer service to meet your customers' needs and provide a positive experience at every interaction with your Shopify store.

2. Setting Up Effective Communication Channels

One of the keys to providing excellent customer service is offering effective communication channels. Shopify provides a variety of options for communicating with your customers, allowing you to address their needs flexibly and conveniently.

Email is a traditional but still effective communication channel. It allows for detailed communication and can be used to send order confirmations, delivery status updates, responses to complex questions, and more. It's also convenient for customers who can read and reply at their own pace.

Live chat is another useful communication channel. It offers real-time interaction, enabling quick issue resolution and answers to questions while the customer is still engaged on your site. Additionally, live chat can provide a more personal experience as customers can have a real-time conversation with a customer service representative.

Social media is also an important communication channel. Many customers already use social media in their daily lives, making it a convenient way for them to reach out to your store.

Social media allows for public communication, which can be an advantage if you provide excellent customer service.

Finally, the phone remains a valuable communication channel. While more communications are moving online, many customers still appreciate the option to speak to a real person over the phone, especially for complex or urgent issues.

When setting up your communication channels, it's important to choose those that best suit your target audience. For example, if your audience is younger, they may prefer social media or live chat. If you sell more complex products, the phone may be a better choice. Once you've selected your channels, it's crucial to manage them effectively to ensure a prompt and consistent response to customer inquiries.

◆ ◆ ◆

3. Responding to Customer Requests and Complaints

When a customer contacts you with a question or complaint, it's crucial to respond quickly, professionally, and empathetically. Every interaction with a customer is an opportunity to strengthen the relationship with them and demonstrate your brand's commitment to excellent service.

Speed is essential. In our connected world, customers expect swift responses. A delay in response can lead to frustration and give the impression that their issue or question is not being taken seriously. That's why it's important to have processes in place for promptly addressing customer requests, whether through email, live chat, social media, or phone.

Professionalism is also critical. Customers expect accurate and informative answers to their questions and effective solutions to their problems. This requires a well-trained customer service team that understands your products, policies, and procedures. Additionally, clear and respectful communication is essential to maintain professionalism.

Empathy is another key component when responding to customer requests and complaints. It's important to understand the customer's perspective and acknowledge the emotions they may be feeling. Empathy can help de-escalate tense situations and make the customer feel heard and valued.

Finally, if you can't immediately resolve the customer's issue, it's important to follow up and keep the customer informed of the situation's progress. This may involve reaching out to other members of your team, contacting the supplier, or conducting additional research. Follow-up demonstrates to the customer that you take their issue seriously and are committed to finding a solution.

By responding to customer requests and complaints quickly, professionally, and empathetically, you can turn a potentially negative situation into a positive experience that strengthens the customer relationship.

4. Handling Returns and Refunds

Handling returns and refunds is an essential part of customer service in e-commerce. Customers appreciate the flexibility and convenience of being able to return or exchange products that don't meet their expectations. Furthermore, a generous return policy can be a determining factor for customers when deciding where to shop.

Shopify makes it easy to manage returns and refunds by offering integrated tools for handling these processes. You can create clear and detailed return policies that are easily accessible to your customers. These policies can include information on the duration during which returns are accepted, the conditions products must meet to be returned, and how customers can initiate a return.

In addition to creating return policies, Shopify allows you to manage refunds directly from your dashboard. You can issue full or partial refunds as needed. When issuing a refund, you can also choose whether to refund shipping fees, which can be a goodwill gesture toward the customer.

It's important to note that effective returns and refunds management also requires excellent communication with the customer. Customers should be informed of the status of their return or refund, and any questions or concerns should be addressed promptly and professionally.

Ultimately, effective returns and refunds management can not only resolve customer issues but also build trust in your brand and long-term customer loyalty. A generous return policy and efficient refunds management can transform a negative experience into a positive one, encouraging customers to continue shopping in your Shopify store.

5. Personalizing the Customer Experience

Personalization is a powerful tool for improving the customer experience and strengthening brand loyalty. By tailoring the shopping experience to each individual customer, you can not only meet their specific needs but also make them feel valued and appreciated.

One way to personalize the customer experience is through personalized communications. This can include using the customer's name in emails, customizing newsletters based on the customer's interests, or sending targeted messages based on the customer's browsing and purchasing behavior. For example, if a customer has recently purchased a certain type of product, you could send them emails showcasing similar or complementary products.

Another way to personalize the experience is by recommending products based on customer preferences and buying behavior. Shopify offers tools that allow you to show customers product recommendations based on what they have viewed or purchased. This not only helps customers discover new products they may love but also increases the average order size.

Finally, you can personalize the customer experience by offering special promotions that are relevant to each customer. For example, you could offer a discount on a product the customer has frequently purchased or provide free shipping to a customer who has spent a certain amount in your store. These special offers can give customers an additional reason to continue shopping in your store.

Personalizing the customer experience may require an investment in time and resources to collect and analyze customer data. However, the benefits in terms of improved customer experience, increased brand loyalty, and higher sales can more than offset this investment.

◆ ◆ ◆

6. Building Customer Loyalty

Building customer loyalty is an essential aspect of running a successful Shopify store. A loyal customer is more likely to make repeat purchases, recommend your store to others, and contribute to the long-term growth of your business. Excellent customer service is one of the most effective ways to build this loyalty.

Excellent customer service goes beyond simply solving problems—it's about creating a positive experience for the customer at every interaction. This can mean responding quickly to questions, going above and beyond to resolve issues, or even surprising and delighting customers with unexpected gestures. When customers feel appreciated and well-treated, they are more likely to remain loyal to your store.

Loyalty programs are another effective tool for building customer loyalty. These programs can reward customers for repeat purchases by offering discounts, gifts, loyalty points, or other benefits. Shopify provides tools that allow you to easily set up and manage loyalty programs.

Special offers can also encourage customer loyalty. This may involve offering exclusive discounts to loyal customers, granting access to special products or services, or providing benefits like free shipping. These special offers can give customers an additional incentive to continue shopping in your store.

Ultimately, building customer loyalty is an ongoing process that requires a commitment to excellent customer service, offers, and programs that reward customers for their loyalty, and a willingness to listen to and respond to customer needs and preferences.

◆ ◆ ◆

7. Measuring Customer Satisfaction

Measuring customer satisfaction is a crucial step in understanding the effectiveness of your customer service efforts and identifying areas that may require improvement. There are several methods for measuring customer satisfaction, each offering unique insights into the customer experience.

Customer satisfaction surveys are a valuable tool for gathering feedback directly from your customers. These surveys can be as simple or as detailed as needed, covering aspects such as the quality of customer service, the ease of using the website, product quality, and more. Surveys can be sent after each customer service interaction or at regular intervals to track changes in customer satisfaction over time.

Product reviews are another valuable source of information about customer satisfaction. By examining reviews left by customers on your products, you can gain insights into what works well and what might need improvement. Positive reviews can indicate your store's strengths, while negative reviews can reveal areas for potential improvement.

Other methods for measuring customer satisfaction may include analyzing customer behavior on your site, such as time spent on the site, bounce rate, and conversion rate. These metrics can provide insights into the overall customer experience when browsing and shopping in your store.

It's important to note that measuring customer satisfaction should be an ongoing activity, not a one-time effort. By regularly measuring customer satisfaction, you can track progress over time, quickly identify issues, and take action to improve the customer experience.

◆ ◆ ◆

8. Success Stories of Shopify Stores with Excellent Customer Service

Examining best practices from other successful Shopify stores can provide valuable insights and effective strategies to improve your own customer service. Here are some examples of Shopify stores that have excelled in providing excellent customer service:

a. Allbirds

Allbirds is a footwear brand known for its commitment to

comfort and sustainability. What truly sets Allbirds apart is its dedication to exceptional customer service. Allbirds offers a generous 30-day return policy, allowing customers to return their shoes for any reason, even if they've been worn. Additionally, Allbirds' customer service team is known for its quick and helpful responses to customer questions and concerns.

b. Gymshark

Gymshark is a sportswear brand that has experienced rapid growth through its online presence. Gymshark has implemented efficient customer service, including live chat on its website, enabling customers to receive instant answers to their questions. Furthermore, Gymshark uses social media to engage with customers, providing another channel for customer service.

c. BlenderBottle

BlenderBottle is a company that sells protein shakers and fitness accessories. BlenderBottle has emphasized providing high-quality customer service, with a dedicated customer service team available via phone, email, and live chat. BlenderBottle also offers a lifetime warranty on its products, demonstrating its commitment to customer satisfaction.

These case studies showcase how different businesses have used available tools and strategies to provide excellent customer service. By examining these examples, you can find ideas and inspiration to enhance your own customer service in your Shopify store.

9. Conclusion

Providing excellent customer service in your Shopify store may seem like a daunting task, but it's an investment that can yield significant dividends in terms of customer loyalty and sales growth. With the right strategies, tools, and a willingness to listen and respond to your customers' needs, you can create an exceptional customer experience that sets your store apart from others.

Excellent customer service begins with a deep understanding of your customers' expectations. In today's digital world, customers expect service that is fast, efficient, personalized, and accessible. By meeting these expectations, you can not only resolve customers' issues but also create a positive experience that strengthens their relationship with your brand.

Effective use of communication channels is also essential for excellent customer service. Whether it's through email, live chat, social media, or phone, each channel offers unique opportunities to interact with your customers and meet their needs.

Handling returns and refunds, personalizing the customer experience, building customer loyalty, and measuring customer satisfaction are other key aspects of excellent customer service. Each of these elements contributes to creating an overall customer experience that encourages customers to return to your store.

Finally, it's important to remember that customer service excellence is not a destination but a journey. It's a process of continuous improvement, where you listen to customer feedback, learn from mistakes, and constantly seek ways to do better. With this mindset, you can transform your customer service into a powerful competitive advantage for your Shopify store.

CHAPTER 15: HOW TO MANAGE RETURNS, REFUNDS, AND CUSTOMER REVIEWS IN YOUR SHOPIFY STORE

Handling returns, refunds, and customer reviews is an essential part of managing an online store. These elements are not just administrative aspects of your business; they are also crucial touchpoints with your customers that can significantly impact their shopping experience.

Returns and refunds are often seen as a negative aspect of running an e-commerce business, but they can also be an opportunity to demonstrate how much you care about customer satisfaction. An easy and transparent return policy can help build trust with your customers, reassuring them that they can return items if they are not satisfied.

Similarly, customer reviews are a valuable resource for any online store. They provide direct feedback on your products and services, allowing you to identify areas where you excel and those that may need improvement. Additionally, positive reviews can serve as a powerful marketing tool, offering social proof that can encourage other potential customers to make a purchase.

However, managing returns, refunds, and customer reviews can be a challenge, especially if you handle a large volume of orders. Fortunately, Shopify offers a range of tools and features that can streamline these processes.

In this chapter, we will explore in detail how you can effectively manage returns, refunds, and customer reviews in your Shopify store. We will cover best practices for establishing return policies, managing return and refund processes, collecting and managing customer reviews, and much more. Whether you are a new store owner or looking to enhance your existing processes, this chapter will provide you with the information you need to manage these crucial aspects of your business efficiently and effectively.

1. Returns and Refund Management

a. Return Policy

The first step in managing returns is to establish a clear and transparent return policy. This policy is more than just a legal document; it is direct communication between you and your customers, defining their rights and your obligations regarding returns.

A well-designed return policy should be easily accessible on your website. You can place it in your footer, main menu, or even include a link to it in your product descriptions and order confirmation emails. The goal is to ensure that customers can find it easily, whether they are making a purchase or considering a return.

Your return policy should detail the conditions under which a product can be returned. This may include information about the types of products that can be returned (e.g., some products like underwear or personalized items may not be eligible for return), the condition products must be in to be returned (e.g., unused, in their original packaging, etc.), and any other specific conditions for your store.

The return process should also be clearly explained in your policy. This can include instructions on how to request a return, how products should be packaged for return, and return shipping information, such as the return address and who is responsible for return shipping costs.

Finally, your return policy should specify return timeframes. Offering a 30-day return window is common, but you can choose to extend or shorten this period based on your business model and products. A clear and transparent return policy can help prevent misunderstandings and conflicts with your customers while building trust in your store. By taking the time to write a detailed and easily understandable return policy, you can streamline the return process for both you and your customers.

b. Return Process in Shopify

Shopify provides built-in tools to manage returns, making it easy to track and handle these transactions for store owners. These tools are designed to be intuitive and user-friendly, even for those new to managing an online store.

To initiate the return process in Shopify, you need to access your store's admin interface. Here, you will find a list of all orders placed in your store. You can search for the specific order you want to return using the order number, customer's name, or other relevant details.

Once you've located the order, you can start the return process by clicking "Create a return." This will open a new page where you can enter the return details.

When creating a return, you will need to specify which items are being returned. Shopify allows you to select the specific items from the order that are being returned, which is particularly useful if only part of the order is being returned. You can also specify the quantity of each item being returned if the customer ordered multiple units of the same product.

In addition to the returned items, you will need to provide a reason for the return. Shopify offers a list of common return reasons that you can choose from, such as "defective item" or "wrong item sent." You can also enter your own reason if none of the predefined options apply to the situation.

The return process in Shopify is designed to be as simple and efficient as possible, allowing you to handle returns quickly and minimize disruptions to your business. By using these tools, you can ensure that your customers receive high-quality return service, which can contribute to their overall satisfaction and loyalty to your brand.

c. Refunds

In addition to returns, managing refunds is another essential part of running your online store. Refunds may be necessary for various reasons, whether it's due to a defective product, an order error, or simply a customer change of mind. Regardless of the reason, it's important to handle refunds efficiently and professionally to maintain customer satisfaction.

In Shopify, the refund process is designed to be as straightforward as possible. To begin, you need to access your store's admin interface and find the specific order you wish to refund. This can be done using the order number, customer's name, or other relevant details.

Once you've located the order, you can initiate the refund process by clicking "Refund." This will open a new page where you can enter the refund details.

When creating a refund, you will need to enter the amount you wish to refund. Shopify allows you to refund the total amount of the order, or you can choose to refund only a portion of the order if it's more appropriate. For example, if only one item from a multi-item order is being returned, you can choose to refund only the cost of that item.

In addition to the refund amount, you will also need to provide a reason for the refund. Similar to returns, Shopify offers a list of common refund reasons that you can select, or you can enter your own reason.

Finally, when creating a refund, you have the option to restock the returned items and notify the customer via email of the refund. Restocking the items automatically adds the returned items back to your inventory, helping you maintain accurate inventory levels. Email notification informs the customer that the refund has been processed, which can help maintain good communication with the customer and reinforce their trust in your store.

By managing refunds efficiently and professionally, you can not only ensure customer satisfaction but also maintain accurate financial management for your store.

2. Customer Review Management

a. Collecting Reviews

Collecting customer reviews is a crucial step in understanding your customers' experience and improving your products and services. Customer reviews provide direct insight into what your customers think of your products, helping you identify strengths and areas for improvement.

Shopify recognizes the importance of customer reviews and offers an integrated product reviews application. This application allows you to collect and manage reviews for your products directly from your Shopify admin interface.

Shopify's product reviews application is designed to be user-friendly. It seamlessly integrates into your store and automatically adds a reviews section to each product page. Customers can leave a review by filling out a simple form on the product page.

In addition to collecting reviews, the application also allows you to moderate reviews. This means you can review each review before it's published on your site, giving you the opportunity to address customer concerns or reject reviews that do not adhere to your guidelines.

The application also offers customization options for the appearance of reviews on your site. You can choose the color, size, and style of the rating stars, and you can even add images or videos to the reviews.

By using Shopify's product reviews application, you can not only gather valuable feedback from your customers but also create a review experience that aligns with your brand and store. Customer reviews can be a powerful marketing tool, and by integrating them professionally and attractively into your site, you can encourage more customers to leave reviews and share their experiences.

b. Review Management

Once you have started collecting reviews, it's important to manage them effectively. Review management goes beyond simply collecting reviews; it includes analyzing, responding to, and using reviews to improve your store.

The first step in review management is to read and understand the reviews. While it may seem obvious, it's essential to take the time to carefully read each review and understand what the customer liked or didn't like. This can provide valuable insights into your product strengths and areas that may need improvement.

Responding to reviews is also an important part of review management. Whether a review is positive or negative, it's always good practice to respond. For positive reviews, a simple thank you can suffice to show the customer that you appreciate their support. For negative reviews, a well-thought-out response can show the customer that you take their concerns seriously and are committed to resolving the issue. In all cases, a response demonstrates that you are attentive to customer feedback and care about their experience.

Finally, it's crucial to use reviews to improve your store. Customer reviews offer direct insights into what works and what doesn't in your store. By taking these feedback points into account, you can make changes to your products, customer service, website, and other aspects of your store to enhance the overall customer experience.

Effective review management can not only improve customer satisfaction but also strengthen your store's reputation and increase sales. By taking the time to properly manage reviews, you can make the most of this valuable resource.

c. Importing and Exporting Reviews

Shopify's product reviews application also offers the ability to import and export product reviews. These features can be extremely useful in various situations, whether you are migrating from another review service, analyzing reviews outside of Shopify, or looking to back up your reviews for security or compliance reasons.

i. Importing Reviews

If you are migrating from another review service or have collected reviews through other means, importing reviews can help you integrate these reviews into your Shopify store. Shopify's product reviews application allows you to import reviews from a CSV file, making it easy to transfer reviews from most other platforms or data formats.

When importing reviews, it's essential to ensure that your data is formatted correctly to be compatible with Shopify's product reviews application. This may include information such as the product name, product ID, customer name, review rating, review title, review text, and review date.

ii. Exporting Reviews

Similarly, exporting reviews can be helpful if you want to analyze your reviews outside of Shopify, create backups of your reviews, or plan to migrate to another platform. Shopify's product reviews application allows you to export your reviews into a CSV file, making them usable in various other applications or platforms.

When exporting reviews, you can choose to export all your

reviews or only a selection of reviews. For example, you can choose to export only reviews for a specific product, only reviews with a certain rating, or only reviews from a specific time period.

By using the import and export features of Shopify's product reviews application, you can manage your reviews in a more flexible and efficient manner, ensuring that you can always access and use your reviews regardless of the context.

3. Conclusion

Effective management of returns, refunds, and customer reviews is a crucial component for the success of your Shopify store. These aspects, though sometimes considered secondary to product sales, are key elements that contribute to overall customer satisfaction and your store's reputation.

By using Shopify's built-in tools, you can simplify and automate many aspects of return and refund management. These tools enable you to process return requests systematically, refund customers quickly, and restock returned items in your inventory, all directly from the Shopify admin interface.

Similarly, Shopify's product reviews application provides you with a platform to collect, manage, and respond to customer reviews. These reviews are a valuable source of information that can help you understand your customers' needs and preferences, improve your products and services, and build trust among customers.

By establishing clear return and refund policies, you can also prevent misunderstandings and reinforce customer trust. A transparent return policy and a fast refund process can make a significant difference in a customer's shopping experience and can even turn a negative experience into a positive one.

Ultimately, effective management of returns, refunds, and customer reviews is a matter of customer service. By focusing on customer satisfaction and doing your best to resolve issues and address concerns, you can not only ensure a positive experience for your customers but also continuously improve your store and increase your chances of long-term success.

CHAPTER 16: HOW TO INCREASE THE AVERAGE ORDER VALUE AND CONVERSION RATE IN YOUR SHOPIFY STORE

In the world of e-commerce, two key indicators play a crucial role in maximizing your Shopify store's revenue: Average Order Value (AOV) and the conversion rate. AOV is the average amount spent by customers each time they place an order in your store. Increasing AOV means increasing the average amount each customer spends, which can have a significant impact on your overall revenue.

On the other hand, the conversion rate is the percentage of visitors to your store who make a purchase. A higher conversion rate means you are more effective at persuading site visitors to take action and become paying customers. It's a key indicator of the effectiveness of your marketing and sales strategy.

These two indicators are closely tied to your overall profitability. By encouraging customers to buy more items per order and converting a larger number of visitors into customers, you can increase your revenue without needing to attract more traffic to your site. It's a more cost-effective and sustainable long-term strategy.

However, increasing AOV and the conversion rate is not an

easy task. It requires a deep understanding of your customer base, a well-designed marketing and sales strategy, and flawless execution. In the following sections, we will explore several strategies you can implement to increase the average order value and conversion rate in your Shopify store.

1.   Increasing Average Order Value

a.   Offering Volume Purchase Discounts

Encouraging volume purchases is a proven strategy to increase the average order value. By offering discounts on volume purchases, you incentivize customers to buy more items each time they place an order, thus increasing the total sales amount.

For example, you can implement a progressive discount structure where the purchase of two items qualifies for a 10% discount, and the purchase of three or more items qualifies for a 20% discount. This creates a sense of urgency and value for the customer, encouraging them to buy more to save more.

Moreover, this strategy can be particularly effective if you sell products that are often purchased together or in multiples. For instance, if you sell beauty products, you can offer a discount on purchasing multiple products from the same range. Or if you sell office supplies, you can offer a discount on buying multiple units of the same item.

It's important to note that this strategy should be implemented thoughtfully. You must ensure that you offer discounts on products with sufficient margins to absorb the discount without harming your profitability. Additionally, communicate the details of the offer clearly to your customers to avoid any confusion.

Ultimately, offering volume purchase discounts is a win-win strategy. It allows customers to feel they are getting a good deal while increasing the average order value for your business.

b. Providing Upsells and Cross-Sells

Upsells and cross-sells are powerful marketing techniques that can significantly boost the average order value in your Shopify store. They not only increase the amount of each sale but also enhance the customer's shopping experience by offering products that add value to their initial purchase.

i. *Upsells*

Upsells involve encouraging customers to purchase a more expensive or higher-end version of a product they have already selected. For example, if a customer is interested in a basic laptop, you can suggest a more advanced model that offers better performance or additional features. The idea is to show the customer how a slightly higher expenditure can bring them significantly greater value.

It's important to exercise tact when proposing upsells. Customers should not feel pressured but rather presented with an option that could better meet their needs. Moreover, it's crucial to offer products that are genuinely relevant to the customer and add value to their purchase.

ii. *Cross-Sells*

Cross-sells, on the other hand, involve encouraging customers to purchase complementary products to the ones they have already chosen. For instance, if a customer buys a dress, you can suggest purchasing matching shoes or a handbag that complements the outfit. Cross-sells can help increase the average order value by enticing customers to make additional purchases they may not have initially planned.

Just like with upsells, cross-sells should be executed thoughtfully. The suggested products should be relevant and add value to the customer's initial purchase. Additionally, it's important not to overwhelm the customer with too many suggestions, as it could make the buying process overly complex and deter the customer from completing their purchase.

By strategically combining upsells and cross-sells, you can raise the average order value while enhancing your customers' shopping experience.

c. Offering Free Shipping for Orders Over a Certain Amount

One of the most effective strategies for increasing the average order value is to offer free shipping for orders that reach a certain threshold. Shipping costs are often a determining factor in a customer's purchase decision. In fact, studies have shown that high shipping fees are one of the main reasons customers abandon their carts. By offering free shipping, you can not only encourage customers to complete their purchase but also add more items to their cart to reach the free shipping threshold.

For example, if you set the free shipping threshold at $50, a customer who has already added items worth $40 to their cart may be incentivized to seek and add another $10 item to qualify for free shipping. This not only increases the value of the current order but can also introduce the customer to another product they may consider purchasing again in the future.

It's important to note that this strategy should be implemented thoughtfully. The free shipping threshold should be set at a level that encourages customers to add more items to their cart but not so high that it discourages purchases. Additionally, you must ensure that you can afford to offer free shipping without negatively impacting your profitability.

In conclusion, offering free shipping for orders over a certain amount is a win-win strategy that can increase the average order value while enhancing customer satisfaction.

2. Increasing the Conversion Rate

a. Optimizing the Product Page

Optimizing the product page is a crucial step in increasing the conversion rate. It's often the point of decision for customers, where they assess the available information and decide whether to add the product to their cart or look elsewhere. Here are some key elements to consider when optimizing your product pages.

i.   Use High-Quality Photos
Product photos are one of the first things customers see when they arrive on a product page. High-quality photos can help create a positive first impression and give customers a good idea of what the product looks like. It's recommended to include multiple photos from different angles and, if possible, photos of the product in use. This allows customers to visualize the product in various contexts and understand how it might fit into their daily life.

ii.   Craft Detailed and Compelling Product Descriptions
Product descriptions play a crucial role in providing customers

with information about the product's features and benefits. A good product description should be both informative and persuasive. It should highlight the key features of the product, explain how it solves a problem or fulfills a customer need, and include words and phrases that evoke emotion and excitement. It's also important to use clear and simple language to ensure customer understanding.

iii. *Emphasize Product Benefits*

In addition to describing the product's features, it's important to highlight the benefits of the product for the customer. This can include elements such as product durability, effectiveness, or how it can improve the customer's life. Emphasizing these benefits can help convince customers of the product's value and encourage them to make a purchase.

iv. *Make the "Add to Cart" Button Visible and Easy to Click*

Finally, the "Add to Cart" button is one of the most critical elements on the product page. It should be clearly visible and easy to click. A "Add to Cart" button that is hard to find or difficult to click can frustrate customers and discourage them from making a purchase. It's recommended to use a contrasting color for the "Add to Cart" button to make it stand out and ensure it's a sufficiently large size for easy clicking, especially for users on mobile devices.

By optimizing these elements of the product page, you can create a more enjoyable shopping experience for your customers and increase the conversion rate of your Shopify store.

b. Simplify the Checkout Process

A smooth and frictionless checkout process is essential for converting visitors into customers. If the process is too complicated or time-consuming, customers may abandon their carts and look elsewhere. Here are some strategies to simplify the checkout process and increase the conversion rate.

i. Offer Multiple Payment Options

Customers appreciate flexibility when it comes to paying for their purchases. By offering multiple payment options, you can accommodate a wider range of customers, including those who prefer credit card payments, debit card payments, PayPal, or even bank transfers. Ensure all transactions are secure to protect your customers' financial information and build trust in your store.

ii. Reduce the Number of Pages or Steps

Every additional step in the checkout process provides customers with an opportunity to change their minds and abandon their purchase. By reducing the number of pages or steps required to complete a purchase, you can make the process faster and easier for your customers, thus increasing the likelihood they will finalize their purchase.

iii. Allow Guest Checkout

Requiring customers to create an account before making a purchase can be a significant barrier. Some customers may not want to take the time to create an account, or they may have concerns about the security of their personal information. By allowing customers to check out as guests, you can eliminate this barrier and make the payment process quicker and easier.

iv. Optimize for Mobile Devices

An increasing number of customers shop on mobile devices, so it's essential that your checkout process is optimized for mobile. This means buttons should be large enough to click easily on a touchscreen, text should be large enough to read on a small screen, and pages should load quickly to avoid keeping customers waiting.

c. Use Clear Calls to Action (CTAs)

Clear and effective calls to action (CTAs) are essential elements of any online marketing strategy. They guide users through the buyer's journey, clearly indicating what they should do next. An effective CTA can significantly increase the conversion rate of your Shopify store. Here are some considerations when creating your CTAs.

i. *Clarity of Message*

A good CTA should be clear and direct. It should precisely indicate what customers should do next and what they can expect in return. For example, "Add to Cart" or "Buy Now" are clear CTAs that specify exactly what the customer should do. Avoid vague or generic terms that could lead to confusion.

ii. *CTA Visibility*

The CTA should be highly visible and stand out from the rest of the page. This means using a contrasting color that grabs attention and placing the CTA where customers are most likely to look for it. For example, the "Add to Cart" button should be positioned near the product image and description, where customers are most likely to find it.

iii. *CTA Size and Design*

The size of the CTA should be large enough to be easily clickable, especially for users on mobile devices. The CTA's design should also be appealing and consistent with your brand. This may include using your brand's colors, fonts, and other design elements.

iv.   CTA Testing and Optimization

Finally, it's crucial to test and optimize your CTAs to maximize their effectiveness. This may involve A/B testing different text, colors, placements, and designs of CTAs to see what works best. Using analytics tools, you can track the performance of your CTAs and make adjustments based on the results.

By using clear and effective calls to action, you can guide customers through the buyer's journey, increase the conversion rate, and ultimately boost sales in your Shopify store.

d.   Provide Excellent Customer Service

Excellent customer service is a crucial element of any thriving business and can have a significant impact on your Shopify store's conversion rate. Quality customer service can reassure customers, address their issues, and answer their questions, all of which can encourage them to complete their purchase. Here are some ways to offer excellent customer service:

i.   Live Chat Support

Offering live chat support on your website can provide instant assistance to customers with questions or concerns. This can help resolve issues in real-time, which can encourage customers to finalize their purchase. Additionally, live chat can provide a more personal and interactive experience, which can help establish a stronger relationship with customers.

ii.   Prompt Response to Customer Emails

Customers appreciate receiving a quick response to their emails. It shows that you take their concerns seriously and are willing to take the time to assist them. Try to respond to customer emails within 24 hours, if possible. If a response to a question requires more time, inform the customer that you have received their email and are working to provide an answer.

iii. Clear and Detailed Return and Refund Policies

Clear and detailed return and refund policies can reassure customers about their purchases. This can be especially important for customers buying expensive items or those uncertain about their purchase. Ensure that your return and refund policies are easily accessible on your website and written in clear and simple language.

iv. Customer Service Staff Training

Make sure your customer service staff is well-trained and capable of addressing customer questions and concerns. They should be knowledgeable about your products, policies, and procedures to provide accurate and helpful responses.

By providing excellent customer service, you can increase customer satisfaction, improve the conversion rate, and build customer loyalty to your brand.

3. Conclusion

Increasing the average order value and conversion rate is a complex task that requires strategic planning and effective implementation. It's a continuous process that requires ongoing attention and regular adjustments to meet the changing needs of your customers and market trends.

The strategies we've discussed, such as offering volume purchase discounts, suggesting upsells and cross-sells, providing free shipping for orders over a certain amount, optimizing product pages, simplifying the checkout process, using clear calls to action, and offering excellent customer service, are all proven methods to increase the average order value and conversion rate.

However, it's important to remember that every Shopify store is unique, and what works for one may not work for another. Therefore, it's crucial to test different strategies, track results, and adjust your tactics accordingly.

Ultimately, the goal is to create a positive shopping experience for your customers that not only encourages them to buy more but also to return for future purchases. By focusing on delivering value to your customers and continually working to improve their experience, you can maximize the revenue of your Shopify store and ensure the long-term success of your dropshipping business.

Finally, remember that success doesn't happen overnight. It takes time, patience, and perseverance to build a thriving dropshipping business. But with a well-thought-out strategy and effective execution, you can increase the average order value and conversion rate, making your Shopify store a success.

CHAPTER 17: HOW TO USE REMARKETING TO INCREASE SALES IN YOUR SHOPIFY STORE

Remarketing, also known as retargeting, is a digital marketing strategy that has revolutionized how businesses interact with potential customers. It is an approach that allows businesses to re-engage with visitors to their website who haven't made a purchase or completed a desired action, such as filling out a form or subscribing to a newsletter.

This strategy relies on the use of cookies, small data files stored on the user's browser, which track the user's online activities and collect information about their browsing habits. This information is then used to present the user with personalized and targeted advertisements when they visit other websites or use mobile applications.

In the context of e-commerce and specifically Shopify, an extensively used e-commerce platform by businesses of all sizes, remarketing can be a powerful tool to increase sales and customer loyalty. By targeting users who have already shown interest in your products or services, you can enhance the relevance of your advertising messages and improve the effectiveness of your marketing efforts.

Furthermore, remarketing can also help increase brand

awareness and strengthen the relationship between the company and the customer. By regularly seeing your brand and products, customers are more likely to remember you and consider your company as a viable option when they are ready to make a purchase.

In summary, remarketing is an essential digital marketing strategy that can help businesses maximize their sales potential, improve their brand awareness, and enhance their relationships with customers.

◆ ◆ ◆

1. What Is Remarketing?

Remarketing, sometimes called retargeting, is a sophisticated digital marketing strategy that presents personalized ads to users who have already visited your website or interacted with your online content. This technique relies on the use of cookies, small data files that are placed on the user's computer or mobile device when they visit your site. These cookies collect information about the user's browsing habits, including the pages they've visited, the products they've viewed, and the actions they've taken on your site.

Once these cookies are set, they allow your business to track the user as they browse the internet. When the user visits other websites that are part of the same advertising network, these cookies signal their presence and trigger the display of targeted ads for your business. These ads can be customized based on the information collected by the cookies, presenting the user with ads directly related to their interests and previous interactions with your site.

Remarketing is a powerful technique because it targets users who have already shown interest in your business, increasing the likelihood that they'll return to your site to make a purchase. Additionally, by presenting personalized ads that are directly related to the user's interests, remarketing can improve the effectiveness of your ads and increase the return on investment for your digital marketing efforts.

In summary, remarketing is a digital marketing strategy that allows businesses to stay top of mind with consumers, improve the relevance of their ads, and enhance the effectiveness of their online marketing efforts.

◆ ◆ ◆

2. Why Is Remarketing Important for Your Shopify Store?

Remarketing is particularly valuable for Shopify stores for several reasons. First and foremost, it enables you to target users who have already expressed interest in your products or services. This means your ads are more likely to be relevant and engaging for these users, increasing the likelihood of them making a purchase. In other words, remarketing allows you to make the most of your existing traffic by re-engaging with users who have already shown interest in your brand.
Additionally, remarketing can boost brand awareness. By regularly displaying ads to users who have visited your site, you can stay top of mind for them. This can be especially useful in

the world of e-commerce, where consumers are often presented with a multitude of options and may easily forget a brand they visited only once.

Remarketing can also increase customer lifetime value. By targeting users who have made a purchase on your site, you can encourage them to return and make additional purchases. This can be highly effective if you use remarketing to present ads for complementary products or special offers that may interest your existing customers.

Lastly, remarketing can help you gather valuable data about your customers. By tracking the browsing habits and buying behaviors of your users, you can obtain valuable insights that can help you refine your marketing strategy and improve the user experience on your site.

In summary, remarketing is an essential tool for any Shopify store looking to maximize its sales potential, increase brand awareness, improve customer loyalty, and gather valuable customer data.

3. How to Implement a Remarketing Strategy for Your Shopify Store?

a. Using Google Remarketing Tools

Google, as one of the biggest players in the digital world, offers a robust suite of remarketing tools that can be integrated with Shopify to maximize your marketing efforts. These tools are designed to help you reach users who have interacted with your website or mobile app by presenting them with personalized ads as they browse the web or use mobile apps.

One of the most popular tools is Google Ads, which offers powerful and flexible remarketing functionality. With Google Ads, you can create remarketing lists based on specific user behaviors on your site. For example, you can target users who have visited a particular product page, added an item to their cart, or made a purchase. These lists can then be used to display targeted ads on Google or other websites that are part of the Google Display Network.

In addition to Google Ads, Google also provides Google Analytics, a tool that can be used to track and analyze user behavior on your site. By integrating Google Analytics with your Shopify store, you can gain valuable insights into how users interact with your site, which can help you fine-tune your remarketing efforts.

Google also offers the option of dynamic remarketing, allowing you to show users ads for products they have previously viewed on your site. This can be particularly effective in encouraging users to return to your site and make a purchase.

In summary, Google's remarketing tools offer a range of options to help you target and reach users who have already shown interest in your Shopify store, increasing the likelihood of conversions and repeat purchases.

b. Using Remarketing on Social Media Platforms

Social media platforms have become an integral part of every business's digital marketing strategy, and remarketing on these platforms can be particularly effective. Many social networks, such as Facebook and Instagram, offer remarketing options that allow you to target users who have visited your site with ads when they use these social networks.

For example, Facebook offers a tool called "Custom Audiences," which enables you to target users who have visited your site or used your mobile app. You can also create "Lookalike Audiences" to reach new users who have similar characteristics to your existing customers. These tools can be used to display targeted ads on Facebook, Instagram, and other sites and apps within the Facebook Audience Network.

Instagram, which is owned by Facebook, also offers similar remarketing options. You can use Instagram's tools to target users who have visited your site with ads when they use Instagram. Additionally, since Instagram is a visual platform, you can use appealing images and videos to capture users' attention and encourage them to return to your site.

In addition to Facebook and Instagram, other social networks like Twitter and LinkedIn also offer remarketing options. These platforms can be particularly useful if your target audience is more likely to use these networks.

By using remarketing on social media, you can not only reach users who have already shown interest in your Shopify store but also leverage the social nature of these platforms to reach new users and increase brand awareness.

c. Using Third-Party Remarketing Tools

In addition to the remarketing options offered by Google and social media platforms, there are also many third-party remarketing tools that can be used with Shopify to further enhance your marketing efforts. These tools may offer additional features, such as the ability to target users based on their behavior on your site, create more personalized ads, or track the performance of your remarketing campaigns in more detail.

Some of the most popular third-party remarketing tools include AdRoll, Criteo, and Retargeter. These platforms offer a range of features that can help you create more effective remarketing campaigns. For example, AdRoll provides behavioral targeting options that allow you to target users based on their actions on your site, such as visiting specific pages or adding products to their cart. Criteo, on the other hand, uses artificial intelligence to optimize your ads and reach users at the most opportune times to encourage them to make a purchase.

Furthermore, these third-party remarketing tools can often be integrated with other marketing tools you use, such as your customer relationship management (CRM) system or marketing automation platform. This can help you create a more cohesive and effective marketing strategy.

In summary, using third-party remarketing tools can offer you more flexibility and control over your remarketing campaigns and help you achieve your marketing goals more effectively. However, it's important to choose a tool that suits your needs and objectives and take the time to understand how to use it to achieve the best results.

4. How to Optimize Your Remarketing Strategy?

a. Segment Your Audience

Segmenting your audience is a crucial step in optimizing your remarketing efforts. By dividing your audience into distinct groups based on specific criteria, you can ensure that you're targeting the right users with the right ads, which can increase the effectiveness of your remarketing campaigns.

For example, you can target users who have added a product to their cart but haven't made a purchase. These users have shown clear interest in a specific product, and targeting them with ads for that product can encourage them to return to your site and complete their purchase.

Similarly, you can target users who have visited a specific page on your site, such as a product category page or a sales page. These users have shown interest in a particular type of product or offer, and targeting them with relevant ads can increase the likelihood of them making a purchase.

Additionally, you can also segment your audience based on demographic criteria such as age, gender, location, or interests. This can help you create more personalized and relevant ads for each segment of your audience.

Remember that audience segmentation is not a one-time action. It's important to regularly review and adjust your audience segments based on the performance of your remarketing campaigns and changes in user behavior.

In summary, audience segmentation is an essential step in optimizing your remarketing efforts. By targeting the right users with the right ads, you can increase the effectiveness of your remarketing campaigns and maximize the return on investment for your marketing efforts.

b. Create Personalized Ads

Personalization is key to the success of any remarketing campaign. By creating ads that are specifically tailored to each user's interests and behaviors, you can increase the effectiveness of your ads and improve the user experience.

For example, you can use dynamic remarketing to show users ads for products they've previously viewed or added to their cart on your site. These ads can remind users of products they liked and encourage them to return to your site to make a purchase.

Additionally, you can personalize your ads by offering discounts or special offers. For instance, you can offer a discount to users who added a product to their cart but didn't complete a purchase or provide free shipping to incentivize them to make a purchase. These offers can be powerful incentives for users to return to your site and complete a purchase.

Furthermore, remember that personalization isn't just about the content of your ads but also their appearance. Use appealing images and designs that reflect your brand and capture the user's attention. Ensure that your ads are optimized for all devices, including desktop computers, tablets, and smartphones.

In summary, creating personalized ads can significantly enhance the effectiveness of your remarketing campaigns. By showing users ads that are directly related to their interests and behaviors, you can increase the relevance of your ads and improve the user experience.

c. Test and Adjust Your Strategy

Like any marketing strategy, it's crucial to test and adjust your remarketing strategy to optimize its effectiveness. The digital marketing landscape is constantly evolving, and what works today may not work tomorrow. Therefore, it's important to take a proactive and flexible approach to managing your remarketing campaigns.

You can test different types of ads to see which ones capture users' attention and encourage them to click. For example, you can test ads with different images, messaging, or calls to action to determine what works best.

Similarly, you can test different audience segments to see which ones are most responsive to your ads. For example, you can test segments based on different user behaviors, demographic criteria, or levels of engagement with your site.

Additionally, you can test different settings for your remarketing campaigns, such as the frequency at which your ads are shown, the timing of their display, or the sites where they are displayed. These settings can have a significant impact on the effectiveness of your ads and should be adjusted based on your campaign's performance.

Finally, remember that testing and adjusting your remarketing strategy should be an ongoing process. User behaviors, market trends, and advertising platform algorithms are constantly changing, and you need to be prepared to adjust your strategy accordingly.

In summary, testing and adjusting your remarketing strategy is a crucial step in optimizing the effectiveness of your campaigns. By taking a proactive and flexible approach, you can ensure that your remarketing strategy remains effective and continues to generate positive results for your business.

5. Conclusion

Remarketing is undoubtedly a powerful tool for boosting sales and customer loyalty in your Shopify store. By targeting users who have already shown interest in your products or interacted with your site, you can increase the relevance of your ads and the likelihood that these users will return to make a purchase. This can not only boost your sales but also improve the user experience, leading to greater long-term customer loyalty.

However, it's important to note that remarketing is not a silver bullet. To be effective, it must be integrated into a broader marketing strategy that includes a clear understanding of your target audience, a strong value proposition, and a website optimized for conversions. Moreover, remarketing must be actively managed and adjusted based on your campaign's performance.

It's also crucial to continue testing and adjusting your remarketing strategy to achieve the best results. This may involve experimenting with different ad types, segmenting your audience in different ways, or adjusting campaign settings to optimize ad effectiveness.

In summary, remarketing is a powerful digital marketing strategy that, when used correctly, can help increase sales and customer loyalty in your Shopify store. However, like any marketing strategy, it's important to approach it thoughtfully, actively manage it, and adjust it based on performance to achieve the best possible results.

CHAPTER 18: ANALYZING AND OPTIMIZING YOUR SHOPIFY STORE'S PERFORMANCE

1. Introduction to Performance Analysis and Optimization

Performance analysis and optimization play a crucial role in the success of your Shopify dropshipping store. By comprehending key data and making informed decisions, you can maximize your chances of success. In this chapter, we will delve into various strategies and tools for evaluating your Shopify store's performance and implementing targeted improvements.

Performance analysis enables you to objectively measure and evaluate your Shopify store's health and performance. By understanding key metrics such as conversion rate, revenue, average order value, and other relevant indicators, you will gain a clear overview of your store's overall performance.

Performance optimization involves identifying areas where improvements can be made to enhance profitability, increase sales, and provide a better customer experience. By analyzing collected data and understanding visitor behaviors, you'll be able to make strategic adjustments to maximize results.

In this chapter, we will guide you through the steps of performance analysis and optimization. We will introduce you to effective tools and methods for data collection and interpretation, providing practical advice for making informed decisions.

Whether you are new to data analysis or seeking to deepen your knowledge, this chapter will equip you with the necessary skills to evaluate your Shopify store's performance and implement strategic improvements. By understanding your store's strengths and weaknesses, you will be able to make informed decisions and shape your business effectively.

Ready to dive into the world of performance analysis and optimization for your Shopify store? Let's continue our exploration to provide you with the knowledge and tools you need to succeed.

◆ ◆ ◆

2. Collecting Data for Your Shopify Store

Before delving into performance analysis for your Shopify store, it's essential to gather relevant data for a clear and accurate understanding of its operation. Here are some key steps to help you get started:

a. Using Google Analytics

Google Analytics is a powerful tool that allows you to track visitor behavior on your site. By integrating Google Analytics with your Shopify store, you can obtain detailed insights into traffic, conversions, traffic sources, visitor behaviors, and more. Be sure to configure Google Analytics correctly by adding the tracking code to your store. This will enable you to collect valuable data on your store's performance.

b. Tracking Key Performance Indicators (KPIs)

Key Performance Indicators (KPIs) are essential measures for assessing the overall health of your Shopify store. They provide a concise view of your store's performance. Some important KPIs include conversion rate, revenue per visitor, average cart value, bounce rate, and page views, among others. Identify the most relevant KPIs for your business and monitor them regularly. These indicators will help you measure progress, identify potential issues, and make informed decisions to optimize your performance.

c. Setting Up Conversion Goals

Conversion goals are specific actions you want visitors to take on your site, such as purchasing a product, signing up for your newsletter, or requesting a quote. Configuring conversion goals in Google Analytics allows you to measure and analyze these actions. This will help you evaluate the effectiveness of your marketing campaigns, landing pages, and conversion processes. Define relevant conversion goals based on your business objectives and track them regularly to assess your performance.

By implementing these data collection steps, you will have a solid foundation for analyzing and optimizing your Shopify store's performance. This valuable information will help you understand how your store is performing, identify strengths and improvement opportunities, and make data-driven strategic decisions.

Let's now move on to the next stage of our exploration, where we will examine how to analyze this data in-depth to gain actionable insights and implement targeted improvements for your Shopify store.

3. Traffic and Visitor Behavior Analysis

Understanding the source of your traffic and how visitors interact with your online store is crucial for optimizing your Shopify store's performance. Here are some key points to consider:

a. Studying Traffic Sources

Analyzing the traffic sources that direct visitors to your Shopify store is essential for optimizing your marketing efforts. Major traffic sources can include organic search, advertising campaigns, social media, email campaigns, inbound links from other websites, and more. Identify the sources generating the most qualified traffic and focus your efforts on them. This will maximize your visibility and attract a relevant audience to your store.

b. Analyzing Visitor Behavior on Your Site

Using analytics tools like Google Analytics allows you to examine visitor behavior on your site. Identify the most visited pages, exit pages, average session duration, bounce rate, and more. This information will help you understand how visitors interact with your store, which pages are most appealing, and which ones need improvement. By analyzing visitor behavior, you can pinpoint the strengths and weaknesses of your Shopify store and make strategic decisions to enhance the user experience.

c. Utilizing Conversion Funnels

Conversion funnels are powerful tools for visualizing the visitor journey from arrival on your site to completing the desired action, such as making a purchase. By analyzing the stages of the purchase process, you can identify friction points where you may lose visitors and make improvements to increase conversions. Identify pages with high abandonment rates and optimize them by simplifying the purchase process, improving the clarity of calls to action, and reducing potential obstacles.

By analyzing traffic and visitor behavior on your Shopify store, you will gain valuable insights to optimize your marketing efforts, improve the user experience, and boost conversions. This data will enable you to make informed decisions and implement targeted improvements to maximize your online store's performance.

◆ ◆ ◆

4. *Product Performance Evaluation*

Evaluating the performance of your products is an essential step in maximizing your sales and profitability within your Shopify store. Here are some key aspects to consider during this evaluation:

a. Analysis of Sales and Revenue per Product

Analyzing sales data allows you to identify which products generate the most revenue in your store. Identify the best-selling products and those that contribute the most to your profitability. By understanding the individual performance of each product, you can determine the factors contributing to their success and use this information to optimize your sales strategies.

b. Identifying the Most Profitable Products

When evaluating the performance of your products, it's essential to consider profit margins. Identify the products that generate the highest margins, even if they are not necessarily the best sellers in terms of revenue. Focus your promotion and showcasing efforts on these profitable products to maximize your profits.

c. Managing Low-Performing Products

If some products fail to meet your sales expectations, it's important to take action promptly. You can consider removing these products from your store or making changes to make them more appealing to your customers. Optimizing your product catalog is essential to maintain a competitive and ever-evolving store. Identify low-performing products and look for improvement opportunities, whether through changes to descriptions, images, prices, or by exploring new products more suitable for your audience.

By regularly evaluating the performance of your products, you will be able to make informed decisions to maximize sales and optimize profitability. A deep understanding of your product assortment will help you remain competitive in the market and offer an attractive shopping experience to your customers.

◆ ◆ ◆

5. User Experience Optimization

User experience is a determining factor for the success of your Shopify store. Here are some key strategies to optimize the user experience and provide a pleasant browsing experience for your visitors:

a. Improving Site Loading Speed

The loading speed of your site is a crucial element for the user experience. Slow loading times can lead to an increased bounce rate, decreased conversions, and visitor frustration. Optimize your site's loading speed by compressing images, using caching, minimizing scripts, and choosing a high-performance host. Ensure that your Shopify store loads quickly on all devices, including mobile, to provide a seamless experience to your visitors.

b. Design and Navigation Optimization

Attractive design and intuitive navigation are essential for delivering an optimal user experience. Ensure that your Shopify store has a clear and appealing layout, with high-quality visuals and consistent color choices. Organize your products into clear categories and offer smooth navigation with well-structured menus. Ensure that visitors can easily find the information they need and access the products that interest them. Simple and intuitive navigation will keep visitors on your site longer and help them quickly find what they're looking for.

c. Using A/B Testing for Page Optimization

A/B testing is an effective method for optimizing your pages and improving conversions. This approach involves comparing different versions of the same page, varying one element at a time, such as the title, images, call-to-action buttons, colors, and more. By conducting A/B tests, you can determine which changes result in a significant improvement in performance. Test different variants, analyze the results, and use the findings to optimize your pages and maximize conversions. A/B testing allows you to take a data-driven approach to make informed decisions about the user experience.

By implementing these user experience optimization strategies, you will create a user-friendly and engaging environment for your visitors, promoting conversions and customer retention. Don't forget to regularly monitor user experience-related metrics, such as bounce rate, time spent on the site, and conversion rates, to identify areas where further improvements can be made.

6. Marketing Performance Analysis

Analyzing the performance of your marketing efforts is essential for effectively allocating your resources and maximizing the results of your Shopify store. Here are some important points to consider during this analysis:

a. Evaluation of Advertising Campaigns

Analyzing the results of your advertising campaigns is crucial to determine their effectiveness and optimize your marketing strategy. Examine key indicators such as click-through rate, cost per click, conversion rate, and return on investment (ROI) for each campaign. Identify campaigns that generate the best ROI and adjust your budgets and strategies accordingly. Focus your resources on the most performing advertising channels and optimize your messages and targeting for the best results.

b. Tracking Return on Investment (ROI)

Measuring the return on investment (ROI) of your various marketing initiatives is essential to assess their financial effectiveness. Calculate ROI by comparing the revenue generated by your marketing activities to the associated costs. This will help you determine the most profitable initiatives and make informed decisions about the allocation of your marketing budget. Identify the channels, campaigns, or actions that offer the best ROI and allocate your resources accordingly to maximize your returns.

c. Using Influencer Marketing to Increase Sales

Influencer marketing can be an effective way to boost sales and amplify your visibility. Analyze the performance of your collaborations with influencers to assess their impact on your Shopify store. Track metrics such as conversion rate, number of generated sales, user engagement, and brand awareness. Identify influencers who deliver the best results and evaluate the profitability of these partnerships. Adapt your influencer marketing strategy based on the results obtained to maximize your impact on your target audience.

By regularly analyzing the performance of your marketing efforts, you will be able to optimize your campaigns, invest your resources efficiently, and maximize the results of your Shopify store. Use data and analytics to make informed decisions, adjust your marketing strategy, and increase the profitability of your promotional activities.

◆ ◆ ◆

7. Using Data for Strategic Decision-Making

The data collected on your Shopify store provides valuable insights that help you make informed strategic decisions. Here are some concrete examples of using data to guide your decisions:

a. Using Data for Pricing Adjustments

Analyzing sales data and profit margins allows you to evaluate the appropriateness of your prices. Identify products that sell well with high profit margins, as well as those that could benefit from price adjustments to stimulate sales. By observing sales trends, you can determine if certain products are overpriced or underpriced relative to market demand. Use this information to make appropriate price changes and optimize the profitability of your Shopify store.

b. Identifying Growth Opportunities

Analyzing sales data and market trends allows you to identify new growth opportunities for your store. By studying emerging market segments, unmet consumer needs, or emerging trends, you can find new perspectives to expand your business. Explore the possibility of targeting new customer segments, developing new products or services, or considering strategic partnerships that will help you drive the growth of your Shopify store. Use data to assess the potential of these opportunities and make informed decisions to maximize your growth.

c. Monitoring Market Trends

Monitoring dropshipping and e-commerce trends is crucial to stay competitive in the market. Use data and analysis to track changes in consumer behavior, new technologies, design trends, product innovations, and more. By understanding these trends, you can adapt your marketing strategy, product offerings, and sales channels to meet the evolving needs of the market. Stay alert to new opportunities and market developments through continuous data analysis.

By using data strategically, you will be able to make informed and responsive decisions to improve the performance of your Shopify store and seize the opportunities that arise. Be sure to collect and regularly analyze relevant data to guide your strategic decisions and maximize the success of your store.

8. Conclusion

In this chapter on the analysis and optimization of your Shopify store's performance, we have explored various strategies and tools to help you evaluate and improve the performance of your dropshipping store. By understanding key data and making decisions based on accurate information, you can maximize your chances of success.

We began by emphasizing the importance of collecting relevant data, focusing on the use of Google Analytics to track visitor behavior, monitor key performance indicators (KPIs), and set conversion goals.

Next, we examined the analysis of traffic and visitor behavior, highlighting the importance of understanding traffic sources, analyzing visitor behavior on your site, and using conversion funnels to improve conversion rates.

We also explored the evaluation of product performance, emphasizing the importance of analyzing sales and revenue per product, identifying the most profitable products, and managing low-performing products.

We then addressed user experience optimization, emphasizing the importance of improving site loading speed, optimizing design and navigation, and using A/B testing for page optimization.

We also highlighted the importance of marketing performance

analysis, focusing on the evaluation of advertising campaigns, tracking return on investment (ROI), and using influencer marketing to increase sales.

Finally, we explored the use of data for strategic decision-making, highlighting pricing adjustments, identifying growth opportunities, and monitoring market trends.

By implementing the strategies and tools presented in this chapter, you will be able to analyze and optimize the performance of your Shopify store in a targeted manner, helping you maximize sales, profitability, and overall success.

CHAPTER 19: MANAGING GROWTH AND CHALLENGES IN RUNNING A SHOPIFY STORE

1. Inventory and Supplier Management

Inventory management is a significant challenge for any e-commerce business, and it becomes even more critical for a dropshipping business. In the dropshipping model, you don't physically own the products you sell, which means you rely on your suppliers to handle inventory. This can pose several challenges.

Firstly, you must ensure that your suppliers have enough stock to meet demand. If a customer places an order for a product that is out of stock with your supplier, it can lead to delays in delivery and a poor customer experience. To avoid this, it's crucial to communicate regularly with your suppliers and understand their inventory management capabilities.

Secondly, you need to be able to track your suppliers' stock levels in real-time. This can be challenging if you work with multiple suppliers or if your suppliers don't have an efficient inventory management system. Fortunately, Shopify offers built-in inventory management tools that can help you monitor your suppliers' stock levels. These tools can alert you when stock levels are low, allowing you to take action to avoid stockouts.

Finally, you must be able to handle returns and refunds efficiently. In the dropshipping model, returns can be complicated because you need to coordinate with the supplier to retrieve the product and process the refund. Again, Shopify offers tools that can assist in managing this process.

In summary, inventory and supplier management are crucial aspects of running a dropshipping Shopify store. By using the right tools and effectively communicating with your suppliers, you can minimize issues and ensure a positive customer experience.

❖ ❖ ❖

2. Maintaining High-Quality Customer Service

As your business grows, maintaining a high level of customer service can become a significant challenge. Rapid growth can lead to an increase in customer service inquiries that may overwhelm your team's capacity to respond effectively and promptly. However, it's crucial to maintain high-quality customer service as it can significantly impact customer satisfaction and loyalty.

Firstly, make sure you have a dedicated team to address customer inquiries and resolve issues. This team should be well-trained and have an in-depth understanding of your products, policies, and processes. They should also be capable of communicating effectively with customers and resolving issues quickly and satisfactorily.

Secondly, invest in tools and technologies that can help your customer service team be more efficient. For example, a Customer Relationship Management (CRM) system can assist your team in tracking customer interactions and managing customer service requests in an organized manner. Chatbots are another useful tool that can be programmed to automatically respond to frequently asked questions, freeing up your team to focus on more complex issues. Chatbots can also be available 24/7, improving customer satisfaction by providing answers to questions at any time.

Finally, it's essential to regularly gather customer feedback on the quality of your customer service. This can help you identify areas for improvement and take actions to enhance your service. You can collect feedback through surveys, social media feedback, or direct discussions with customers.

In summary, maintaining high-quality customer service as your business grows can be a challenge, but with a dedicated team, the right tools, and a constant focus on improvement, you can continue to provide excellent service to your customers.

3. Managing Returns and Refunds

Returns and refunds are an inevitable part of e-commerce. They can be a source of frustration for customers and stress for businesses. However, effective management of returns and refunds can transform these challenges into opportunities to improve customer satisfaction and brand loyalty.

Firstly, it's crucial to establish a clear and fair return policy. This policy should be easily accessible and understandable for customers. It should outline the conditions under which a product can be returned, the return process, and the type of refund the customer can expect (e.g., a full refund, store credit, etc.). A fair return policy can not only help resolve issues efficiently but also build trust between you and your customers.

Secondly, ensure that your customer service team is well-trained to handle returns and refunds. They should have a deep understanding of your return policy and be able to communicate it clearly to customers. They should also be capable of handling challenging situations with tact and professionalism, always keeping the goal of customer satisfaction in mind.

Thirdly, consider investing in tools or software that can automate and streamline the return process. For example, some tools can automatically generate return labels for customers, making the process easier for both them and you.

Finally, use returns and refunds as an opportunity to learn and improve. Analyze the reasons for returns to identify potential issues with your products or order process. Use this information to make improvements that can reduce the number of returns in the future.

In summary, while managing returns and refunds can be a challenge, a proactive and customer-focused approach can help turn this challenge into an opportunity to enhance your business.

◆ ◆ ◆

4. Conversion Optimization and Increasing Average Order Value

As your traffic increases, optimizing your conversion rate becomes increasingly important. A higher conversion rate means you're getting more out of the traffic you generate, which can lead to a significant increase in sales and revenue.

Conversion optimization begins with understanding your customers and their journey on your site. Use analytics tools to track user behavior on your site and identify friction points that may prevent them from converting. For example, a complicated checkout process or insufficient product information can deter customers from placing an order.

Once you've identified friction points, test different elements of your site to see what works best. This can include call-to-action buttons, product images, product descriptions, page layout, and more. A/B testing can be an effective way to determine which changes lead to an increase in the conversion rate.

In addition to conversion optimization, you should also seek to increase the average order value. This means encouraging customers to spend more with each purchase. There are several techniques for achieving this, such as upselling and cross-selling. Upselling encourages customers to buy a higher-priced or premium version of a product, while cross-selling encourages customers to purchase complementary products.

For example, if you sell computers, an upsell could be encouraging customers to buy a model with more memory or a faster processor. Cross-selling could involve encouraging customers to buy a mouse or laptop bag in addition to their computer purchase.

In summary, conversion optimization and increasing the

average order value are two key strategies for maximizing the revenue of your Shopify store. By understanding your customers, testing different elements of your site, and encouraging customers to spend more, you can boost your sales and revenue.

◆ ◆ ◆

5. Performance Analysis and Optimization

Performance analysis and optimization are essential elements of managing and growing a Shopify store. By understanding how users interact with your store and identifying areas for improvement, you can make changes that increase engagement, enhance the user experience, and ultimately boost sales.

One of the most powerful tools at your disposal for performance analysis is Google Analytics. This free tool allows you to track a wide range of metrics, including the number of visitors to your site, bounce rate, time spent on the site, conversion rate, and more. You can also see where your visitors come from, which pages they visit, and the path they take to make a purchase.

This information can help you identify areas where you can improve. For example, a high bounce rate may indicate that visitors are not finding what they're looking for on your site or that they find the site difficult to navigate. In such cases, you might consider redesigning your site layout or improving the clarity of your product information.

Additionally, if you notice that visitors spend very little time on your site, it could indicate a lack of engagement. You might consider adding more interactive content, such as product videos or customer reviews, to encourage visitors to spend more time on your site.

In addition to Google Analytics, Shopify also offers its own integrated analytics tools. These tools can help you track sales, orders, and visitor trends directly from your Shopify dashboard.

In summary, performance analysis and optimization are ongoing processes that can help you understand your customers, improve your store, and increase sales. By using analytics tools and making adjustments based on your findings, you can continue to enhance and expand your Shopify store.

6. *International Growth Management*

International growth can be an exciting step for any e-commerce business. However, it also comes with many unique challenges that require careful planning and preparation.

One of the first challenges is translating your site. This involves not only translating the text on your site into another language but also ensuring that the tone, style, and cultural context are appropriate for the target audience. Working with professional translators or native speakers can be helpful to ensure that your content is well-received by international customers.

In addition to translation, it's important to understand cultural differences that can affect how international customers perceive and interact with your store. Preferences in design, buying habits, and customer service expectations can vary significantly from one country to another. Researching the target market and adapting your store accordingly can help increase engagement and sales.

Compliance with local laws and regulations is another significant challenge in international expansion. This may include consumer protection laws, data privacy regulations, product labeling requirements, and more. It's crucial to understand these laws and ensure that your store is compliant to avoid fines or legal disputes.

Finally, consider the logistical aspects of international expansion. This may include managing international shipments, handling currency exchange rates, and setting up payment systems that accept foreign currencies.

In summary, managing international growth is a complex process that requires thorough planning and research. However, with the right strategy and tools, you can overcome these challenges and open your Shopify store to a much larger global audience.

7. Conclusion

Managing the growth of a Shopify store is a complex process that involves many challenges. Whether it's inventory and supplier management, maintaining high-quality customer service, managing returns and refunds, optimizing conversion rates, increasing average order values, analyzing and optimizing performance, or handling international growth, each aspect requires careful attention and a well-thought-out strategy.

However, these challenges should not be seen as insurmountable obstacles but rather as opportunities for learning and growth. With the right strategies, appropriate tools, and a proactive approach, you can overcome them and continue to expand your business.

It's important to note that growth doesn't happen overnight. It's a process that requires time, patience, and perseverance. It's also essential to remain flexible and open to change, as the world of e-commerce evolves rapidly.

Finally, remember that the success of a Shopify store is not only measured in terms of sales or revenue but also in terms of customer satisfaction, brand loyalty, and reputation in the market. By keeping these factors in mind and constantly striving for improvement, you can not only manage the growth of your Shopify store but also lead it to sustainable success.

CHAPTER 20: HOW TO STAY UPDATED WITH DROPSHIPPING TRENDS

Dropshipping is a constantly evolving business field characterized by rapid dynamics and continuous changes. In this context, the ability to stay up-to-date with the latest trends is not only beneficial but essential to maintain the competitiveness of your Shopify store.

Market trends, whether they concern new popular products, changing consumer preferences, or new marketing strategies, can change quickly and unpredictably. What's popular and profitable today may not be so tomorrow, and vice versa. Therefore, constant market monitoring is necessary to stay ahead and not fall behind competitors.

However, following trends doesn't just mean being aware of what's currently happening in the industry. It also involves anticipating future changes and adjusting your strategy accordingly. This may include adding new products to your store, changing your marketing strategy, or even redesigning your website to reflect the latest consumer trends and preferences.

In the end, staying updated with dropshipping trends is a complex task that requires constant monitoring, in-depth analysis, and the ability to adapt quickly. However, those who manage to do so will be well-positioned to capitalize on opportunities and ensure the long-term success and growth of their Shopify store.

1. Understanding the Importance of Trends

Dropshipping trends play a crucial role in determining the success of your business. They can influence many aspects of your operation, from product selection to marketing strategy, supplier choices, and website design.

For example, if a certain product category becomes popular, it may be wise to consider adding it to your store. This could not only increase your sales but also attract a new segment of customers to your shop. Furthermore, adding popular products can improve your store's visibility on search engines, potentially leading to increased traffic and sales.

Similarly, if a new social media platform gains popularity, you may consider using it for your marketing efforts. Social media platforms are excellent tools for reaching and engaging with your target audience. By using a popular platform, you can expand your marketing reach, enhance customer engagement, and ultimately increase sales.

However, it's important to note that following trends doesn't necessarily mean adopting all of them. Some trends may not be relevant to your business or target audience. Therefore, it's crucial to evaluate each trend based on its potential impact on your business before deciding to adopt it.

In the end, understanding the importance of trends and knowing how to leverage them to your advantage can help you stay competitive in the dynamic landscape of dropshipping.

2. Monitoring Market Trends

In the ever-changing world of dropshipping, monitoring market trends is an absolute necessity. Fortunately, there are many ways to do so, thanks to various tools and resources available.

One of the most effective methods for tracking trends is to use market research tools like Google Trends. This tool allows you to see search trends for different products and categories, giving you a clear idea of what consumers are currently searching for. You can use this information to anticipate demand and add relevant products to your store.

In addition to Google Trends, there are other market research tools that can help you track trends. For example, tools like SEMRush and Ahrefs can provide insights into popular keywords and trending topics in your niche.

Furthermore, following industry blogs, forums, and news sites can help you stay updated with the latest industry news and trends. These sources can provide valuable information about changes in the industry, new technologies, and effective marketing strategies.

Lastly, social media is another excellent way to track trends. By following relevant influencers, joining industry groups, and monitoring popular hashtags, you can get real-time insights into what's trending.

It's important to note that monitoring market trends requires constant effort. Trends can change rapidly, and what's popular today may not be tomorrow. Therefore, dedicating time each day to market monitoring and adapting your strategy accordingly is crucial.

3. Analyzing Dropshipping Trends

Analyzing dropshipping trends is a crucial step that goes beyond simply observing market movements. It involves thorough evaluation and interpretation of data to make informed decisions that can significantly impact your business.

When analyzing trends, it's important to consider a variety of factors. For instance, an increase in the popularity of health and wellness products may indicate a growing awareness of health and wellness among consumers. This could be an opportunity to add similar products to your store, catering to the rising demand and attracting a new segment of customers.

However, it's not just about adding popular products to your store. It's also important to understand why these products are popular and how they fit into the broader market context. For example, if these products are popular due to a short-term trend, they may not be a good long-term option.

Similarly, if you notice a decline in the popularity of electronic products, it could indicate a shift in consumer preferences or market saturation. In this case, you may consider reducing your stock of these products or finding ways to differentiate them from your competitors.

Analyzing dropshipping trends may also involve examining sales data, customer feedback, and the performance of similar products on different platforms. By combining this information, you can get a more comprehensive picture of market trends and make more informed decisions for your business.

In the end, analyzing dropshipping trends is an essential skill for any dropshipping entrepreneur. By understanding market trends and adapting your strategy accordingly, you can stay competitive and ensure the long-term growth of your business.

◆ ◆ ◆

4. Adapting Your Strategy to Trends

Once you've identified and analyzed dropshipping trends, the next step is to adapt your strategy accordingly. This adaptation is a dynamic process that requires strategic thinking and effective implementation.

Adding new products to your store is one of the most direct ways to adapt your strategy. If you've identified a growing trend for certain types of products, adding them to your store can help you capitalize on the trend and increase your sales. However, it's important to exercise discernment when adding new products. Ensure that these products align with your brand and target audience and that they are of high quality.

Modifying your marketing strategy is another way to adapt to trends. For example, if you notice that your target audience is increasingly using a particular social media platform, you can adjust your marketing strategy to include that platform. Similarly, if a certain marketing technique becomes more effective in your industry, such as influencer marketing or content marketing, you can incorporate it into your marketing strategy.

Finally, updating your website to reflect the latest trends can also be an effective strategy. This may involve updating your website design to align with web design trends, adding new features that have become popular, or even redesigning your website to better meet customer expectations.

It's important to note that adapting your strategy to trends should be a thoughtful process. It's not about following every new trend that emerges but choosing the ones that make the most sense for your business and can help you achieve your long-term goals. By staying flexible and being ready to adapt, you can successfully navigate the ever-evolving landscape of dropshipping.

◆ ◆ ◆

5. Examples of Dropshipping Trends

To illustrate how to track and analyze dropshipping trends, let's examine some recent trends that have had a significant impact on the market.

a. Health and Wellness Products

The COVID-19 pandemic has led to a significant increase in demand for health and wellness products. Consumers have become more aware of the importance of maintaining good health and overall well-being, leading to increased demand for everything from dietary supplements to home fitness equipment. Products that support mental well-being, such as meditation kits or relaxation products, have also seen an increase in demand. By analyzing this trend, you could consider adding a range of health and wellness products to your store to meet this growing demand.

b. Sustainable Products

There is a growing trend towards sustainable and eco-friendly products. Consumers are increasingly conscious of the environmental impact of their purchases and seek to support businesses that share their ecological values. This includes everything from natural beauty products to eco-friendly household items to clothing made from recycled materials. By following this trend, you could consider offering a range of sustainable products in your store to attract environmentally-conscious consumers.

c. Pet Products

Pet products are always popular, and this trend is expected to continue in the future. With a growing number of people owning pets, the demand for everything from pet toys to pet health products has increased. Furthermore, as pets become more humanized, owners seek high-quality and personalized products for their pets. By following this trend, you could consider adding a range of pet products to your store to meet this growing demand.

These examples illustrate how dropshipping trends can vary significantly, covering different products, categories, and consumer behaviors. By tracking and analyzing these trends, you can adapt your dropshipping strategy to take advantage of these market opportunities.

6. Conclusion

Staying updated with dropshipping trends is more than just a recommendation; it's an imperative necessity for the success of your Shopify store. The e-commerce landscape is in constant flux, with new trends, technologies, and consumer behaviors constantly emerging. To remain competitive, you must be able to navigate this dynamic landscape and adjust your business accordingly.

Regularly monitoring and analyzing market trends is an essential part of this adaptation. It allows you to understand what consumers want, how their behaviors are changing, and which products or services are currently in demand. With this information, you can make informed choices about which products to stock, which marketing strategies to employ, and how to present your store to attract and retain customers.

However, staying updated with dropshipping trends doesn't mean simply reacting to every new trend that emerges. It's also about discerning passing trends from enduring changes and making strategic choices that support the long-term growth of your business. This may mean ignoring some trends, even if they are popular, if they don't align with your brand or target audience.

In the end, staying updated with dropshipping trends is an ongoing process that requires constant vigilance, in-depth analysis, and a willingness to experiment and innovate. By doing so, you can ensure that your Shopify store remains competitive, relevant, and appealing to customers, both today and in the future.

CHAPTER 21: CONCLUSION; HOW TO SUCCEED WITH A DROPSHIPPING SHOPIFY STORE

Congratulations! You've reached the end of this learning journey dedicated to dropshipping with Shopify. Throughout the chapters, we've explored the many facets of this form of e-commerce, from creating your online store to optimizing your marketing strategy, selecting your products, and managing your customer service.

Today, we're ready to conclude this journey. But before we turn the final page, let's take a moment to reflect on all that we've accomplished. Each chapter in this course was designed to provide you with the tools and knowledge needed to build and manage a successful dropshipping business. You've learned how to navigate the Shopify ecosystem, choose the right products and suppliers, optimize your store for SEO, and much more.

This final chapter aims to consolidate all the knowledge you've gained. It's about connecting the various elements we've covered and showing you how they fit into an overall vision of success. We'll revisit some key concepts, share inspiring success stories, and provide practical tips for applying what you've learned to your own dropshipping business.

But more than anything, this chapter is here to remind you that dropshipping is not just about selling products online. It's about providing value to your customers, creating a strong brand, and building a sustainable business. With the right strategies and a good dose of determination, you have everything it takes to succeed in your dropshipping business. So, are you ready for this final step? Let's go!

◆ ◆ ◆

1. Success Stories

The world of dropshipping is filled with success stories that can serve as a source of inspiration and motivation. These entrepreneurs started just like you, with an idea and the determination to succeed. Their journeys perfectly illustrate how the concepts and strategies we've discussed throughout this course can be put into practice to create a thriving dropshipping business.

Take, for example, the story of Irwin Dominguez, an entrepreneur based in California. With no prior experience in e-commerce, Irwin managed to generate over a million dollars in revenue in just eight months after launching his dropshipping business. How did he achieve this feat? By applying the basic principles of dropshipping we've discussed: finding a profitable niche, selecting the right products, creating an attractive online store, and implementing an effective marketing strategy.

But Irwin is not the only one who has experienced such success. There's also the story of Tim Kock, who created a dropshipping store that generated $6,667 in just 8 weeks. Tim used a different approach, focusing on building a strong brand and using influencer marketing to attract customers.

And then there's the story of Sarah, a single mother who turned a small dropshipping store into a thriving business that now allows her to live comfortably and support her family. Sarah emphasized excellent customer service and product quality to stand out from the competition.

These success stories show that there isn't just one "right" way to succeed in dropshipping. Each entrepreneur used a unique combination of strategies and tactics to achieve their goals. What's important is understanding the basics of dropshipping, knowing your market and customers, and being ready to work hard and learn from your mistakes. With these elements in place, you have every chance of joining the ranks of these successful entrepreneurs.

2. Key Elements to Master for Success

a. Adding Value

In the competitive world of dropshipping, simply selling products is not enough to stand out and build a successful business. It's essential to add value for your customers beyond the basic transaction.

This can be done in several ways. Firstly, by providing quality information. This can take the form of detailed and informative product descriptions, blogs or articles on topics relevant to your niche, or guides and tutorials that help your customers make the most of their purchases. For example, if you sell fitness equipment, you could create workout guides, exercise demonstration videos, or articles on nutrition and wellness. These contents add value by helping your customers reach their goals and strengthening their trust in your brand.

Secondly, you can add value by solving your customers' problems. This may involve responding quickly and effectively to customer questions and concerns, providing assistance with delivery or product issues, or offering innovative solutions to meet your customers' specific needs. For example, if you sell electronic products, you could offer technical support or troubleshooting guides to help customers resolve common issues.

Finally, you can add value by offering unique products that cater to your customers' specific needs. This may involve selecting niche products that aren't readily available elsewhere, creating your own products or exclusive designs, or customizing your products based on your customers' preferences. For example, if you sell jewelry, you could offer customization options like engraving names or special messages.

In summary, adding value for your customers means going beyond simply selling products. It's about creating a positive shopping experience, addressing your customers' needs and desires, and building a long-term relationship that encourages loyalty and repeat purchases.

b. Marketing and SEO

Traffic is the lifeblood of any e-commerce business. Without visitors browsing your products and making purchases, your online store simply cannot thrive. That's why it's essential to master different marketing strategies and understand the role of SEO (Search Engine Optimization) in attracting visitors to your store.

Marketing for your dropshipping store can take many forms. It can include social media marketing, where you use platforms like Facebook, Instagram, and Pinterest to reach your target audience and encourage them to visit your store. It can also include email marketing, where you build a subscriber list and regularly send them updates about new products, promotions, and other store news.

Influencer marketing is another powerful strategy, where you collaborate with influencers in your niche to promote your products to their audience. And of course, there's paid advertising, where you use platforms like Google AdWords or Facebook Ads to reach a broader audience.

Alongside these marketing efforts, SEO plays a crucial role in driving visitors to your store. SEO involves optimizing your store and product listings for search engines, so when people search for products like yours, they find your store in search results. This can involve using relevant keywords in your product descriptions, optimizing your site's structure for search engines, and creating high-quality content that can attract links to your site.

In summary, marketing and SEO are two essential aspects of running a successful dropshipping store. By mastering these skills, you can attract a steady stream of visitors to your store, increase your online visibility, and ultimately boost your sales and profits.

c. Specialization

In the world of dropshipping, choosing to specialize in a specific product or niche can give you a significant competitive advantage. Instead of trying to sell a little bit of everything to everyone, specialization allows you to focus on the specific needs of your target audience and position yourself as an expert in your field.

Specialization can take several forms. For example, you can choose to focus on a specific type of product, such as eco-friendly yoga clothing, vintage photography accessories, or educational toys for children. By concentrating on a specific type of product, you can deepen your knowledge of that product, understand what makes a good product in that area, and select the best products for your store.

Alternatively, you can specialize in a specific market niche. For example, you might decide to target yoga enthusiasts, amateur photographers, or parents of preschool children. By focusing on a specific market niche, you can better understand the needs, desires, and challenges of that group and select products that specifically cater to those needs.

Specialization can also help you stand out from the competition. In a crowded market, being perceived as an expert in a specific field can help you gain customers' trust and build a strong brand. Furthermore, by focusing on a specific niche, you can often avoid direct competition with large retailers and general e-commerce sites.

In summary, specialization is a powerful strategy for success in dropshipping. By choosing to focus on a specific product or niche, you can better serve your customers, stand out from the competition, and position your store for long-term success.

d. Long-Term Perspective

It's important to understand that dropshipping is not a get-rich-quick scheme. Like any business, building a successful dropshipping business takes time, patience, and perseverance. It's essential to adopt a long-term perspective and not be discouraged if you don't see immediate results.

Dropshipping, like any other business, has its own challenges and obstacles. There may be periods of slow sales, issues with suppliers, technical problems with your online store, and many other challenges. However, these challenges are not insurmountable. With perseverance, continuous learning, and a willingness to adjust and improve your strategy, you can overcome these obstacles and build a thriving business.

Moreover, it's important not to focus solely on short-term sales. While generating sales is, of course, important, it's also essential to build long-term relationships with your customers. This may involve providing excellent customer service, creating a strong and appealing brand, and working on customer retention. Loyal customers who come back again and again can be a valuable source of long-term revenue for your business.

Finally, it's crucial to continue learning and growing as an entrepreneur. The world of e-commerce and dropshipping is constantly evolving, with new trends, tools, and strategies emerging regularly. By staying up-to-date with these developments and constantly seeking to improve your skills and knowledge, you can ensure that your business remains competitive in the long run.

In summary, success in dropshipping requires a long-term perspective. It takes patience, perseverance, and a willingness to learn and adapt. Don't be discouraged if you don't see immediate results – with time and effort, you can build a prosperous dropshipping business.

e. Exceptional Customer Service

In the world of e-commerce, excellent customer service is not only desirable but absolutely essential. It can make the difference between a business that survives and one that thrives. Exceptional customer service can help you build a good reputation, retain customers, and generate repeat business.

Exceptional customer service starts with clear and prompt

communication. Customers appreciate quick responses to their questions or concerns. Whether it's through email, live chat, or social media, make sure to respond promptly to customer inquiries. Even if you can't immediately resolve an issue, a quick response to inform the customer that you're working on their request can go a long way in building trust.

Efficiently resolving issues is also crucial. This may involve working with your suppliers to resolve delivery issues, handling returns and refunds fairly, or offering innovative solutions to address specific customer needs. Remember that each problem resolved to the customer's satisfaction can turn a dissatisfied customer into a brand advocate.

But exceptional customer service isn't limited to problem management. It's also about creating a positive experience for your customers at every stage of the buying process. This can involve providing detailed and accurate product descriptions, making the ordering process as simple and smooth as possible, and following up with thank-you emails or personalized offers after the purchase.

Finally, remember that customer service is an opportunity to learn from your customers. Customer feedback and input can provide valuable insights into your products and store, helping you identify areas where you can improve.

In summary, exceptional customer service is a key element of success in dropshipping. By responding promptly to customer inquiries, resolving issues effectively, and constantly working to improve the customer experience, you can build a strong reputation and retain customers for repeat business.

f. Avoiding Analysis Paralysis

In the world of dropshipping, there are numerous decisions to make – what niche to choose, what products to sell, how to market your store, and much more. With so many variables to consider, it can be easy to fall into the trap of "analysis paralysis," where you spend so much time analyzing and pondering your options that you end up not taking any action at all.

It's important to understand that perfection is not attainable, and uncertainty is part of entrepreneurship. While it's essential to do your research and plan carefully, at some point, you need to make a decision and take action. Whether it's choosing a product, launching a marketing campaign, or addressing a customer service issue, action is often the best remedy for analysis paralysis.

Furthermore, remember that mistakes are an inevitable and valuable part of the learning process. Every error or failure is an opportunity to learn and improve. If a particular approach doesn't work, you can always adjust your strategy and try something new. In fact, the ability to quickly learn from your mistakes and pivot accordingly is one of the most valuable skills a dropshipping entrepreneur can possess.

In summary, don't let analysis paralysis hold you back. Do your research, plan carefully, but remember that action is the key to progress. Make decisions, learn from your mistakes, and don't be afraid to adjust your strategy along the way. With this approach, you can continue to move forward, learn, and grow as a dropshipping entrepreneur.

3. Common FAQs

Dropshipping, like any other business model, is surrounded by many misconceptions and frequently asked questions. These misconceptions can often discourage new entrepreneurs or lead them to make decisions based on incorrect information. Here are some of the most common misconceptions about dropshipping, and the truth behind them.

a. Dropshipping is not profitable

This is probably one of the most common misconceptions about dropshipping. The truth is that, like any other business, the profitability of dropshipping depends on many factors, including product selection, pricing strategy, cost management, and the effectiveness of marketing. With the right strategy and efficient execution, dropshipping can certainly be a highly profitable business.

b. It's too late to start dropshipping

Some people think that because dropshipping is a popular business model, the market is saturated, and it's too late to start. However, while dropshipping has become more competitive over the years, there are still plenty of opportunities for those willing to do the necessary research and find unique product niches. Furthermore, e-commerce continues to grow every year, meaning more and more customers are shopping online.

c. Dropshipping is easy

Another common misconception is that dropshipping is an

easy way to make money online. While dropshipping has some advantages, such as not needing to manage physical inventory, it also comes with its own challenges. It requires thorough market research, excellent customer relationship management, an effective marketing strategy, and the ability to handle logistical issues and supplier problems.

d. All products can be dropshipped

While dropshipping offers great flexibility in terms of the types of products you can sell, not all products are ideal for dropshipping. For example, products that are very heavy or bulky may not be profitable to dropship due to high shipping costs. Similarly, products that require a lot of after-sales service or technical support may also not be ideal for dropshipping.

In summary, it's important to do your own research and understand the realities of dropshipping before getting started. With a good understanding of the business model and a solid strategy, dropshipping can be an excellent way to start an online business.

4. Additional Resources

To further deepen your knowledge of dropshipping, SEO, marketing, and other aspects of e-commerce, here is a list of valuable online resources:

- **Shopify Blog:** For e-commerce and dropshipping tips.

- **Moz Blog:** To learn about SEO.
- **HubSpot Blog:** For digital marketing.
- **Ahrefs Blog:** Another excellent resource for SEO and content marketing.
- **Neil Patel's Blog:** For advanced digital marketing strategies.
- **Ecommerce Fuel:** For e-commerce tips for 6 and 7-figure businesses.
- **Oberlo Blog:** Specifically for dropshipping.
- **Ecommerce Bytes:** For e-commerce news and information.
- **Reddit r/dropship:** A community forum for dropshippers.
- **Google Digital Garage:** For free courses on digital marketing.
- **Coursera and Udemy:** For online courses on e-commerce, SEO, and marketing.
- **Google Trends:** To identify product trends.
- **AliExpress Dropshipping Center:** To find products to dropship.
- **DigitalMarketer Blog:** For advanced digital marketing strategies.
- **Search Engine Journal:** For SEO and SEM tips and news.
- **Social Media Examiner:** For social media marketing strategies.
- **Kissmetrics Blog:** For information on analytics and tracking data.
- **Practical Ecommerce:** For practical e-commerce advice.
- **Yotpo Blog:** For customer retention and reviews tips.
- **Ecom Elites Blog:** For dropshipping and e-commerce advice.
- **Reddit r/ecommerce:** Another community forum for e-commerce entrepreneurs.
- **LinkedIn Learning:** For online courses on e-commerce, SEO, and marketing.

- **Skillshare:** For online courses on various e-commerce-related topics.
- **Jungle Scout Blog:** For tips on selling on Amazon.
- **SaleHoo Blog:** For dropshipping and wholesale selling tips.
- **Ecomdash Blog:** For inventory management and shipping tips.
- **Alibaba Insights:** For market trends and supplier information.
- **Google Keyword Planner:** For keyword research for SEO.

These resources can help you stay updated with the latest trends and strategies in the ever-evolving world of e-commerce.

5. Conclusion

In conclusion, dropshipping is an extraordinary entrepreneurial adventure, a true odyssey into the fascinating world of e-commerce. It's a business that can be launched with a modest initial investment but has the potential to offer impressive returns. It's a unique opportunity to dive into the dynamic world of e-commerce, discover new markets, and connect customers from around the world with the products they're looking for.

Through this course, you have gained a wealth of valuable knowledge and skills. You've learned how to create and manage your own Shopify store, how to select the right products and suppliers, how to optimize your site for SEO, how to implement effective marketing strategies, and much more.

And now, the moment has come! It's time to take action

and launch your own dropshipping business. The world of e-commerce is eagerly awaiting you. Yes, it's normal and even expected to have fears and doubts when embarking on something new and unknown. But don't let these fears hold you back from realizing your dreams. Remember, every failure is a step toward success, an opportunity to learn, grow, and improve.

Dropshipping is not a get-rich-quick scheme; it's an adventure that requires time, effort, and perseverance. There will be challenges and obstacles along the way, but with determination and a willingness to learn, you can overcome them. And most importantly, don't forget to enjoy the process. After all, entrepreneurship is not just about profits but also about passion and personal fulfillment.

Celebrate every success, big or small. Every sale, every positive feedback from a customer, every goal achieved is a validation of your hard work and determination. These moments of success are precious and deserve to be celebrated.

The world of e-commerce is constantly evolving, with new trends, technologies, and opportunities emerging all the time. To succeed, it's essential to stay curious, keep learning, and adapt to changes.

The journey to success in dropshipping may be challenging, but it's also incredibly rewarding. With the knowledge you've gained in this course, you're well-prepared to start your journey. So, don't hesitate any longer, take the plunge, and pursue your entrepreneurial dreams. We look forward to seeing what you'll accomplish. Good luck and enjoy the exciting adventure!

◆ ◆ ◆

GLOSSARY

1. **Dropshipping:** A business model where the retailer does not keep products in stock but transfers customer orders to the manufacturer or another retailer.
2. **Shopify:** An e-commerce platform that allows you to create an online store and sell products.
3. **Niche:** A specific segment of the market characterized by a particular target group or specialized product.
4. **Dropshipping supplier:** A company that produces and/or stocks products and then ships them directly to the customer on behalf of the dropshipping retailer.
5. **SEO (Search Engine Optimization):** Techniques used to improve a website's ranking in search engine results.
6. **Google Analytics:** A free service from Google that allows tracking and reporting of website traffic.
7. **Facebook Pixel:** Code placed on a website to track conversions from Facebook ads, create audiences for future ads, and remarket to people who have already taken action on the website.
8. **Email marketing:** A form of direct marketing that uses email to promote a company's products or services.
9. **Influencer marketing:** A form of social marketing that uses endorsements and product mentions from individuals with a dedicated social following.
10. **Customer service:** Assistance and guidance that a company provides to those who buy or use its

products or services.
11. **Average Order Value (AOV):** The average total amount spent each time a customer places an order on a website or mobile app.
12. **Conversion rate:** The percentage of website visitors who complete the desired action.
13. **Remarketing:** A marketing strategy that targets people who have previously visited your website but did not take the desired action.
14. **Dropshipping trends:** Changes and developments in the world of dropshipping that can impact how you run your business.
15. **Online payment:** A transaction conducted through the internet involving the exchange of electronic funds.
16. **Shipping:** The process of sending goods from the supplier to the customer.
17. **Shopify theme:** Design template for Shopify stores.
18. **Store optimization:** The process of improving the efficiency and effectiveness of an online store.
19. **Google Ads:** An online advertising platform where advertisers pay to display ads, service listings, product listings, videos, and more.
20. **Facebook Ads:** An advertising platform that allows businesses to create targeted ads to reach different audiences.
21. **Instagram Ads:** Ads that appear on Instagram and can be targeted based on various demographic and behavioral factors.
22. **Paid advertising:** A form of advertising where businesses pay to display their ads on various platforms.
23. **Returns:** The process by which customers return purchased products.
24. **Refunds:** The return of money to a customer following a product return or dissatisfaction.

25. **Customer reviews:** Feedback left by customers about the products or services they have purchased.
26. **Upselling:** Sales technique where the seller encourages the customer to buy a more expensive product, upgrade, or another item to make the sale more profitable.
27. **Cross-selling:** Sales technique where the seller encourages the customer to buy complementary or related products.
28. **Performance analysis:** The process of evaluating the effectiveness and efficiency of a business.
29. **Growth management:** Strategies and practices for managing and supporting business growth.
30. **Management challenges:** Problems and obstacles managers face when running a business.
31. **Market trends:** Movements and developments in the market that can affect a business.
32. **Marketing strategy:** An action plan designed to promote and sell products or services.
33. **Social media marketing:** The use of social media platforms to promote a product or service.
34. **Return policy:** Rules and procedures established by a company to manage product returns by customers.
35. **Refund management:** The process of returning money to a customer following a product return or dissatisfaction.
36. **Customer reviews management:** The process of collecting, managing, and responding to customer reviews.
37. **Inventory:** The total quantity of goods and/or materials that a business has on hand at a given time.
38. **High-margin products:** Products that generate a high profit margin relative to their cost.
39. **Low-margin products:** Products that generate a low

profit margin relative to their cost.
40. **Trending products:** Products that are currently popular or in fashion.
41. **Seasonal products:** Products that are popular or in demand during specific seasons or times of the year.
42. **Evergreen products:** Products that maintain their popularity and demand over time, regardless of trends or seasons.
43. **Niche products:** Products intended to serve a specific market segment or target group.
44. **Mass-market products:** Products intended to serve a wide audience or a large market segment.
45. **B2B (Business to Business):** Commercial transactions between two businesses, such as between a manufacturer and a wholesaler, or between a wholesaler and a retailer.
46. **B2C (Business to Consumer):** Commercial transactions between a business and an end consumer.
47. **C2C (Consumer to Consumer):** Commercial transactions between two consumers, typically facilitated by a third-party platform.
48. **E-commerce:** The activity of buying or selling goods or services online.
49. **M-commerce:** The buying and selling of goods and services through wireless mobile devices.
50. **Logistics:** The management of warehousing and distribution of goods.
51. **Shipping costs:** The expense associated with shipping an item from one location to another.
52. **Free shipping:** Shipping service where the company absorbs the shipping costs, so the customer does not have to pay for shipping.
53. **Express delivery:** Fast shipping service that guarantees product delivery in a shorter time than standard delivery.

54. **Standard delivery:** Shipping service that does not offer fast delivery but is generally cheaper than express delivery.
55. **Deferred delivery:** Shipping service where the customer chooses a future delivery date.
56. **Pickup point delivery:** Shipping service where the customer retrieves their order at a specific location rather than receiving it at home.
57. **Home delivery:** Shipping service where products are delivered directly to the customer's residence.
58. **Click and Collect:** Service where customers can purchase products online and pick them up in-store.
59. **Marketplace:** An online platform where products from different sellers are sold.
60. **Payment service provider:** A company that provides online payment processing services to merchants.
61. **Secure payment:** Payment made through a system that protects credit card information and other sensitive data.
62. **Installment payment:** Payment option that allows customers to pay for their purchases in multiple installments over a period.
63. **Cash on delivery:** Payment option where the customer pays for products upon delivery.
64. **Payment on order:** Payment option where the customer pays for products when placing the order.
65. **Deferred payment:** Payment option that allows customers to receive a product before paying for it.
66. **Credit card:** Payment method that allows cardholders to pay for goods and services based on a promise to pay for them.
67. **Paypal:** An online payment service that allows individuals and businesses to transfer funds electronically.
68. **Bank transfer:** The transfer of funds from one bank

account to another.
69. **Check:** A document instructing a bank to pay a specific sum from the writer's account to a person or business.
70. **Cryptocurrency:** A type of digital currency that uses cryptography to secure transactions and control the creation of new units.
71. **Shopping cart:** Interface on an e-commerce website that allows users to place items they wish to purchase.
72. **Product page:** A page on an e-commerce website that provides details about a specific product.
73. **Home page:** The first page a visitor sees when arriving on a website.
74. **Category page:** A page on an e-commerce website that displays a list of products within a certain category.
75. **Contact page:** A page on a website that provides information on how to contact the company.
76. **About Us page:** A page on a website that provides information about the company.
77. **Blog:** A section of a website that contains articles, typically written by the company or website owner.
78. **Newsletter:** Regular email bulletin sent to subscribers.
79. **Pop-up:** A type of window that opens without user interaction when visiting a website.
80. **Banner:** A large advertising panel placed on a website.
81. **Slider:** A graphical element that displays multiple items (usually images) in a rotating sequence.
82. **Footer:** The bottom section of a website page that typically contains company contact information, links to company policies, etc.
83. **Header:** The top section of a website page that typically contains the company logo, navigation

menu, etc.
84. **Navigation menu:** A menu bar or list of links that helps visitors navigate a website.
85. **Search filters:** Tools that help users refine their search results on a website.
86. **Internal search engine:** A tool that allows users to search for specific content on a website.
87. **Live chat:** A service that enables users to communicate in real-time on a website.
88. **FAQ (Frequently Asked Questions):** A page on a website that contains answers to commonly asked questions.
89. **Terms and Conditions (T&Cs):** A document that defines the terms and conditions under which a company sells its products or services to customers.
90. **Legal notices:** Information required by law to be provided on a website, typically related to the company's identity, site terms of use, etc.
91. **Privacy policy:** A document explaining how a company collects, uses, and manages user data.
92. **Cookies:** Small data files stored on a user's computer by a website, typically used to track user preferences and browsing activities.
93. **Back office:** The part of an enterprise information system used to manage operations not directly related to customers, such as inventory and order management.
94. **Front office:** The part of an enterprise information system that manages direct interactions with customers, such as the company's website and customer service.
95. **CMS (Content Management System):** Software that allows users to create, manage, and edit website content without needing specialized technical knowledge.
96. **CRM (Customer Relationship Management):**

Software that helps businesses manage and analyze interactions with their customers.

97. **ERP (Enterprise Resource Planning):** Software that helps businesses manage and integrate critical parts of their operations.
98. **PIM (Product Information Management):** Software that helps businesses manage all the information needed to market and sell products.
99. **DMP (Data Management Platform):** A platform that collects, organizes, and activates data from various sources.
100. **KPI (Key Performance Indicator):** A measure used to evaluate the success of an organization or a specific activity.

Printed in Great Britain
by Amazon